*f*P

MY LOVE AFFAIR WITH AMERICA

THE CAUTIONARY TALE OF A CHEERFUL CONSERVATIVE

NORMAN PODHORETZ

The Free Press

New York London Toronto Sydney Singapore

f**P**

THE FREE PRESS
A Division of Simon & Schuster Inc.
1230 Avenue of the Americas
New York, NY 10020

THE FREE PRESS and colophon are trademarks
of Simon & Schuster Inc.

Designed by Jeanette Olender
Manufactured in the United States of America

1   3   5   7   9   10   8   6   4   2

LIBRARY OF CONGRESS CATALOGING-IN-PUBLICATION DATA

Podhoretz, Norman.
My love affair with America: the cautionary tale of a
cheerful conservative / Norman Podhoretz.
p.   cm.
Includes index.
1. National characteristics, American.   2. United States—Politics and
government—Philosophy.   3. United States—Politics and government—1945–1989.
4. United States—Politics and government—1989–.   5. Patriotism—United States.
6. Conservatism—United States.   7. Podhoretz, Norman.
8. Intellectuals—United States—Biography.   I. Title.
E169.12.P59 2000   99-462225
320.52'0973—dc21

ISBN 0-7432-0051-9

My son John Podhoretz
not only gave me the idea for this book
but then also made invaluable editorial suggestions,
and I dedicate it to him in the same spirit of love
and gratitude in which I wrote it.

CONTENTS

O beautiful for spacious skies,
For amber waves of grain,
For purple mountain majesties
Above the fruited plain!
America! America!
God shed his grace on thee
And crown thy good with brotherhood
From sea to shining sea!

—From "America the Beautiful"
by Katharine Lee Bates (1893)

"God's Country"

As far back as the eighteenth century, the great literary critic and lexicographer Dr. Samuel Johnson, a fervent Tory who might have been expected to think otherwise, famously dismissed patriotism—to give love of country its proper name—as "the last refuge of a scoundrel." And for at least the past hundred years, patriotism has been treated even more derisively by American writers and intellectuals than it was by the towering Englishman who came before them. It has been associated not only with scoundrels but with charlatans, demagogues, fools, nativist bigots, and the "boosterism" that H. L. Mencken, Sinclair Lewis, and so many others once mercilessly ridiculed to such lasting effect.

Nationalism, a related though distinct phenomenon, has perhaps fared even worse. Since it suggests pride in, more than love of, country and carries with it besides an intimation of defiant bellicosity which at its extreme edges becomes jingoism or chauvinism, nationalism has often been excoriated as the main cause of war. There was a time, for example, when it (rather than, say, the character and traditions of the German people or the grievances arising from the Treaty of Versailles or the mysteriously persistent power of anti-Semitism) was widely blamed for the rise of Nazism.

On the other hand, love of country, and pride in it, is so common a feeling among peoples everywhere in the world that there seems something almost fatuous, if not positively perverse, about making an issue of it. Celebrating or condemning patriotism, and even nationalism, is rather like praising or deploring human nature itself. After all, even a lifelong radical like the philosopher

Bertrand Russell could say of his own country that "Love of England is very nearly the strongest emotion I possess."

I feel much the same way about America, land of my birth, "land that I love." (I can still hear those words being belted out every week on the radio by Kate Smith, a big star of the 1940s, in her signature song, "God Bless America.") But I only plumbed the depths of this feeling in the course of being driven, almost against my will, to defend the country with all my might against its ideological enemies on the Left from the late 1960s on. These were people who had been my own political allies and personal friends up to the point where they were seized by a veritable hatred of America; and it was because I could not stomach the terrible and untrue things they were saying about this country that I wound up breaking with them.

Eventually, with a pit stop or two along the way, I sought and found refuge on the Right, not least because its attitude toward America was in complete harmony with my own. But then, in the mid-1990s, there unexpectedly came an outburst of anti-Americanism even among some of the very conservatives I thought had been permanently immunized against it. I should have known better than to be surprised, familiar as I was with the traditions on which the conservatives were drawing and which they were now updating. These were traditions that had mostly originated in America itself in the period after the Civil War, but reinforcements had also been imported from Europe (where, by the way, anti-Americanism was just now enjoying a resurgence evidently fueled by resentment of the fact that the United States had been left by the fall of the Soviet Union as the only "superpower" in the world).

The motives and the issues behind this outburst on the Right in America had little if anything in common with the ones that had formerly animated the Left (and that lived on in various disguises and mutations such as bilingualism and multiculturalism). To my sorrow and dismay, however, the end result was uncomfortably similar in a disheartening number of respects.

What to do? The truth is that I encountered a stiff inner resistance to buckling on my slightly rusted armor for yet another campaign: "Why should the agéd eagle stretch its wings?" Edmund Wilson, commenting in his critical classic of the 1930s, *Axel's Castle*, on that very line from T. S. Eliot's great poem "Ash Wednesday," said that it made him "a little tired at hearing Eliot, [then] only in his early forties, present himself as an 'agéd eagle' who asks why he should make the effort to stretch his wings." But when those words of Eliot popped into my own head, I was already pushing seventy, and it made *me* a little tired to think of going back into combat over a phenomenon that I had fondly imagined I would never have to deal with again, and certainly not on the Right. Unable, however, to help myself, back I went anyway. Fortunately for my tattered ensign, this new round had a very much shorter duration than the first and did not (I hope!) leave me, as its predecessor had, with a new set of ex-friends.

Another stroke of good luck from my point of view was that I did not feel the same obligation to open up a second front by replaying the struggle against the latest wave of European anti-Americanism. An older version had occupied me as a young student in England nearly a half-century earlier, when an even more virulent resentment over the predominance of American power in the aftermath of the Second World War had become pervasive throughout Europe. But I was living in America now, I no longer visited Europe much, and this time I was more than content to let that particular cup pass from my lips.

Yet the resurrection of anti-Americanism on the Right in America itself also turned out, perversely, to be a stroke of luck. From my point of view, it was (if I may be permitted a small sacrilege) a *felix culpa* on the part of the Right, in that my being summoned from the reserves into active duty, and having to defend this country once more, served to remind me of why I loved it so much. In addition, it refreshed my sense of why (unlike, say, England or France) America was always being denigrated and defamed. And it also helped me realize why merely rebutting these attacks in a polemical mode, as I had spent much of my adult life doing, was not enough. Beyond being defended by a counterattack against its assailants and an exposure of their misrepresentations and slanders, America deserved to be glorified with a full throat and a whole heart.

That is exactly what I want to do here through telling—and with only as much polemic as is needed (again a line from T. S. Eliot pops into my mind) "to swell a progress, start a scene or two," or set a context—the story of how and why my love affair with America developed, how it ran into a rough patch, and how it then emerged with all doubts stilled and reservations removed, leaving me uncharacteristically full of optimism and good cheer. America, according to some who have preceded me in their attitude toward it, is "God's country." This is, as the pages that follow will attest, a judgment with which I have no inclination whatsoever to disagree.

PART

I

"Who Is He, That Uncle Sam?"

It all began with language.

I was born in this country, in the Brownsville section of Brooklyn, but as a very small child I spoke—or so family tradition has it—more Yiddish than English. My father, Julius Podhoretz,*[1] had been here for eighteen years and my mother, Helen (neé Henyeh),[2] for ten when I came along in 1930, and they both knew English reasonably well. But my paternal grandmother, Runyeh,[3] lived with us when I was little, and she barely spoke English at all despite the fact that she too had been here for quite a long while. The same was true of my other three grandparents, all of whom, in accordance with the invariable custom in their generation, were in marriages that had been arranged by their parents without consulting them.

These marriages, incidentally, had been duly solemnized by rabbis "in accordance with the law of Moses and of Israel," but in the pre–World War One era, few East European Jews bothered getting them ratified by the state, to whose authority in such matters they were largely indifferent. In the eyes of civil officialdom, therefore, their children (that is, the immediate ancestors of the vast majority of American Jews stemming from that part of the world) were legally considered bastards. Hence when these children were issued passports, the documents would bear the surnames of their mothers.

---

*The derivations of this and all other Jewish names mentioned below can be found in the numbered endnotes beginning on p. 237.

Unaware of this, and presumably never having inspected the papers she had carried with her, my own mother suffered a great shock upon arriving at Ellis Island in 1920 at age seventeen. Expecting to be met by her father, M'shitzik[4] Woliner, who had gone to America before the war broke out and had been cut off for six years from his family in Galicia (then a province of the Austro-Hungarian Empire), she waited and waited and waited as "Henyeh Werker" kept being summoned to be picked up. Finally, she was the only one left in the cavernous hall. She had been a little girl when her father last laid eyes on her, but peering through the gate he realized that the lone young woman standing there disconsolately was his daughter, and when she was then allowed through the gate, he reintroduced himself not with an embrace or a kiss but by yelling at her for failing to come forward. At this display of her father's characteristic mode of address, she burst into tears and told him that she thought her name was "Henyeh Woliner," not Henyeh Werker. (In America, though the "Henyeh" soon became Helen, she would as often be referred to by the former as by the latter.)

There is another story connected with my mother's arrival in America that I cannot resist telling here, so powerfully does it capture the wonders of the America I love and have set out to glorify, but it requires fast-forwarding all the way from 1920 to 1950. That was when I was graduated from Columbia University, which I had attended for four years on a scholarship endowed by Joseph Pulitzer—a Jew from Hungary who had come to this country much earlier than any member of my family and had grown rich and powerful as a newspaper publisher. Now, having partaken of the fruits of Pulitzer's success in America, I was about to embark for Cambridge University in England on a fellowship endowed not by a Jew but by a quintessentially American WASP lady named Euretta J. Kellett.

Two Kellett fellowships, one for Cambridge and one for Oxford, were awarded every year by Columbia, and in 1950 the Oxford-bound winner was someone named Emmanuel Chill, whom I had never met. In those days, the Kellett was considered an important enough award to be announced in the *New York Times*, with pictures of the two Fellows included in the story. "You know," my mother said upon reading the *Times* piece, "when I came to America, an older girl named Ida Chiel* from my village was on the same ship, going to join her husband, who was the son of Mendel Chiel. She already knew a little English, and during the trip she taught me to say, 'How do you do, my dear father,' so I could greet him like a regular American when we landed" (an effort which, as we have seen, turned out to be sadly wasted under the circumstances). "Anyway, I lost touch with her after a while, but I'll bet Emmanuel Chill is her son, named after Mendel. Probably this Emmanuel takes after Mendel too, because he was very educated. He could even understand the Polish newspapers, and so he was the one we all depended on to bring us news during the war. I remember how we would all get together in the marketplace every week to hear him read in a loud voice with his big glasses on his nose."

To this I responded impatiently, "For Godsakes, Mom, I don't even know if the guy is Jewish. Anyway, it's too crazy." Undeterred, she announced she was going to telephone Emmanuel Chill's mother. "Don't you dare!" I shouted, deeply embarrassed. But behind my back, she dug up the number, which turned out to be listed in the Bronx phone book, and when a woman's voice answered, my mother said, "Mrs. Chill," this time using the soft "ch," which she was capable of pronouncing when she wanted to, "I'm the other mother and I'm calling to congratulate you."

After Mrs. Chill had politely thanked her, my mother, not missing a beat, asked her if "by any chance" her first name was Ida. And

---

*She pronounced the "Ch" as "kh"—a hard and guttural sound that does not exist in English.

of course it was, and of course this "other mother" was the very same Ida Chiel with whom mine had traveled to America, where, after drifting apart, they would both live as members of the working class. Yet America had found two of their sons there, plucked them up, and deposited them into a great university in which Jews were still only grudgingly welcomed (the unacknowledged Jewish quota at Columbia until the late 1950s was 17 percent of the total undergraduate population). To top it all off, a mere thirty years after these two young girls from a tiny hamlet in East Europe had crossed the Atlantic in steerage and landed on Ellis Island, America was sending their two sons back across the same ocean, only now in grand style and to a very different part and level of the continent.

The name of Harry Golden is no longer much remembered, but this Jew from the Lower East Side of Manhattan, who moved to North Carolina and became a very popular newspaperman down there, wrote a big best-seller in the early 1960s whose title by itself summarizes the theme that unites this story with a thousand others of similar, if less melodramatic, impact: *Only in America.**

Back now to the other side of my family and why my father's mother Runyeh lived with us when I was little. It was not, as one might think, because she had become a widow. Her husband,

---

*"Only in America" became the tag line of many good jokes and stories. Thus, when the Lord Mayor of Dublin came to visit New York, and Casey Stengel (or was it Yogi Berra?) of the Yankees learned that this high official of the capital of Ireland was Jewish, he is alleged to have shaken his head in wonderment and said in all seriousness, "Only in America." I am tempted to say the same thing about the proximity of the two villages—Podgorecz and Rogatyn—from which I and the financier and diplomat Felix Rohatyn each got our names (though he himself was born in Vienna before emigrating to the United States as a child escaping from the Nazis.)

my other grandfather, Yidl[5] Podhoretz, to whom she had presented five sons while they were still in Europe, was very much alive when she left him not long after their arrival in America. Allegedly the breakup resulted from disputes over the distribution of his "*paydeh*," which was a new Yiddish coinage, derived from the English "pay day," that came to be used by many immigrants to describe the family finances.

Naturally there was more to it than that. Dark rumors circulated that Runyeh held Yidl partly responsible for the suicide of her youngest sister Perel,[6] who had leaped to her death from the window of the fifth-story cold-water flat she had been sharing with them in a tenement building on the Lower East Side of Manhattan. Perel had a clubfoot and was very homely to boot, but she had been rescued from spinsterhood by being married off in Europe to a hapless and totally penniless cousin when she was in her late twenties and he was only about nineteen.

With her new husband, *der schvartzer* Yankl[7] ("the black Yankl") —meaning not that he was swarthy but that he had dark hair and was thereby distinguishable from another of their cousins, *der roiter* Yankl, whose hair was red—Perel had a baby. This baby would become Nathan Podhurst in America, where he would work all his life as a shipping clerk in one of the factories that made up New York's bustling garment center. But despite being in this lowly occupation, Nathan would see nothing incongruous about getting an endless supply of "business cards" printed up for him. These he would distribute with a great flourish even to his close relatives, including the little children among them, announcing every time he did so: "Here is Nathan Podhurst, with a capital N and a capital P."*

But this was many years in the future. When Nathan was still an infant, with nary a capital letter to his name, his father *der*

---

*He pronounced his own name with a Yiddish accent as "Nayt'n Podhoist." As for why it was Podhurst rather than Podhoretz, see endnote 1 on page 237.

schvartzer Yankl fled to America, where (like my grandfather M'shitzik) he was happily stuck by the outbreak of the First World War. When the war ended, Perel followed after, but Yankl, older now, less docile, and wised up by his exposure to the freer ways of America, refused to resume living with her, and she moved in with my grandparents. No amount of pressure or cajoling from the family could make Yankl change his mind and take her back. Becoming as a result more and more despondent, Perel finally committed suicide.

It was probably because my grandfather Yidl had been insufficiently sympathetic to her pathetic youngest sister, and not because of disputes over *paydeh*, that Runyeh left him. And it was entirely characteristic of my family that the explanation offered for Perel's suicide should have been as bowdlerized (for the sake not only of the children but of themselves too) as the one offered for Runyeh's breakup of her marriage. Perel, they said, trying to dye her hair with henna, had put on too much, and the result was an itching so intense that it drove her first crazy and then out of the window. Even as a kid, I smelled something fishy in this story. But I thought it the better part of prudence to let sleeping legends lie. Anyway, probing into this one would have been a useless exercise, since it was inconceivable that a truthful account would ever be forthcoming.

Similarly in Runyeh's own case: one day, whatever the cause, she packed up her stuff, including the huge pots and pans she had carted over with her from Europe. Thus encumbered, she and her youngest son, my uncle Meyer, then in his late teens, moved without so much as a by-your-leave into our small apartment in Brooklyn where, as my mother would still be complaining with undiminished resentment sixty or more years later, there was no room in our overstuffed cupboards for those pots and pans. Runyeh also forbade her husband to visit. Hence poor Yidl—as they told me when I grew old enough to be let in on such stories—was forced to take many endless trolley rides from lower Manhattan to Brooklyn and hover secretly across the street from our apartment building in order to catch a glimpse of the infant grandson (me) he adored but could never again embrace.

It goes—or should go—without saying that leaving her husband did not mean that Runyeh had changed her mind about the institution of marriage. To be sure, even if she had wanted a divorce, it would have been virtually impossible for her to get one under Jewish law (to which she was strictly faithful) unless her husband agreed to give it to her; and Yidl, who evidently harbored dreams of reconciliation, would never hear of it. But in truth, she had no desire for a divorce, either; nor did she wish to remarry when her husband died.

What she did want was to become an American citizen, and she wanted it passionately enough to spend many months boning up with the help of my only sibling, my big sister Millie—five years older than I—on the facts about which she expected to be quizzed by the judge. Who was the first President?; what was the Constitution?; who freed the slaves?: these were the things to which she memorized the answers, rehearsing them in her painfully broken English. At last the great day came. But the judge, who must surely have been an anti-Semite, asked this elderly and obviously religious Jewish woman only one question: "Madame, do you believe in bigamy?" Imagining, probably, that bigamy was one of the principles of the American Constitution to which she was about to swear fealty, Runyeh instantly answered, "Sure,* judge," and that was that.

Bewildered by her rejection, she turned to my mother, her daughter-in-law, who had accompanied her to the hearing, and asked in Yiddish what she had done wrong. Upon being given the explanation, her indignation reached about as high a pitch as any human being could experience without bursting into a thousand

---

*A word she pronounced as "Shoo-a."

pieces. "That scoundrel!" she exclaimed, "*me* he asks such a question?!" Thus it was in a bizarre connection with marriage—a kind of divine retribution, as she may well in the secret recesses of her heart have taken it, for her own sins against the institution—that her ambition to become an American citizen was frustrated.

Yidl died in 1934 when I was four years old, and I remember him only well enough to know that he was infinitely more loving and tender than my other grandfather M'shitzik. In this, M'shitzik was not all that unusual. Indeed, men like him were sufficiently common in the culture of East European Jewry to have a designation of their own—he was *a bayzer Yid*, an angry Jew—though I doubt that another so perfectly realized a specimen of the type ever existed. He might make a rare exception in the case of his granddaughters and my mother, but neither his other two daughters nor his two sons nor I or any of his other male grandchildren were ever on the receiving end of so much as a smile.

And it got worse as he became more and more religious. Strictly Orthodox to begin with, he grew with the passage of the years in America (during most of which he worked as the *shammes*, or sexton, of a musty old Brooklyn synagogue) into an ultra—what in Israel would come to be called a *haredi*.* Later, when I got to know a bit about these matters, I realized with a jolt one day that he was not very learned, and I used to joke that since the 613 commandments binding upon a pious Jew were not enough for him, he had invented new ones, like a prohibition against whistling, which he was firmly convinced had been ordained by God.

Not surprisingly, then, it was just as far from roses in the mar-

*Literally, a "trembler"—before God, of course.

riage department for my mother's parents as it was for my father's. Which is to say that M'shitzik and Esther Malkah never "got along," either. This was the euphemism employed by my mother, the eldest of *their* five children, to describe what was in fact a loathing so intense that husband and wife literally ceased speaking to each other until death did them part (she went first in an accident when I was in my teens, and he passed away about twenty years later, shortly after settling in a *haredi* community in Israel). But not content with refusing to speak to each other, they also spoke against each other, even to their own grandchildren.

Once, for example, M'shitzik warned my sister Millie, then about eight or nine, not to eat anything her grandmother might feed her when she visited, since it might well be poisoned. (In view of the fact that what Esther Malkah fed her was Millie's favorite sandwich—which consisted of sliced radishes and raw onions smothered in chicken fat between two pieces of heavy black pumpernickel bread, with a side dish of extremely sour pickles—he may inadvertently have had a point.)

Unlike my father's parents, however, M'shitzik and Esther Malkah never actually separated once they were reunited in marital misery after being apart during the years of the war. M'shitzik seemed to prefer seething to splitting up, and Esther Malkah was too timid to leave him. Instead, she spent as much time as she possibly could hiding from him in our apartment, thus replacing on a part-time basis my other grandmother Runyeh, who was eventually installed in an apartment of her own right around the corner from ours. There Runyeh contracted cancer and then followed her estranged husband Yidl into the grave only four years after he died of a bronchial infection that he might have survived if his spirit had not been too broken to fight.

These tangled domestic arrangements were totally at variance with the sentimental picture that later developed of that generation of pious Orthodox Jews: the men with their full beards and sidecurls, dressed in long black coats and hats to match,* and the women with their unadorned ankle-length dresses and *shaytlach* (the wigs—cheap, rarely washed, and often smelling unpleasant—that married women were required to wear), which was exactly what all four of my grandparents looked like. Unusual or not, the poisonous marital relations between both sets of my grandparents had an indirect and lasting effect on me, deriving from the fact that none of them ever learned much English or bothered trying to speak it.

But before explaining how and why this turned out to be so consequential for me, I cannot resist fast-forwarding once again to another highly evocative story, this one about my maternal grandmother Esther Malkah.

Being unable to speak English did not mean that she was totally ignorant of it. Once in a while—sometimes with comical results, sometimes not—she would even throw an English word or two into a Yiddish sentence. The most extraordinary example I can think of was her exclamation upon hearing on the big Zenith console radio in our living room the slogan "Uncle Sam Needs You." This was during the Second World War, and her youngest son, my uncle Maxie, had just been drafted, an event to which she responded as yet another of the great calamities that life cruelly refused to cease visiting upon her. Was it not enough that she had been left by her horrible husband to fend for herself and their five little children through the bombardments preceding the conquest of their village back "home" in Galicia by the Cossacks and the

*It would have surprised most of these men to learn that their sartorial fashions, which the less learned took for granted as having been prescribed by Jewish law, had actually come down to them from neither the Bible nor the Talmud but from the way Polish and Russian noblemen had dressed in the Middle Ages.

daily hunger that accompanied the Russian occupation of it?* (Too weak and depressed to bear up under these hardships, she had made a habit of passing out every Friday night before the onset of the Sabbath, thereby leaving my humiliated but brassy preteen mother to run shouting through the village, "Mama just fainted again, please come help.") With all that behind her, did she now have to endure the anxiety of waiting to hear that her youngest son had been killed in yet another war?

It was just too much, and so turning to me sitting next to her on the couch, she cried: "*Ver iz er, der Uncle Sam? Im hob ikh extra in dr'erd!*" ("Who is he, that Uncle Sam? Him I would especially like to send six feet under.") I suspect that adding the English word "extra" seemed to her to make the familiar Yiddish curse (literally, "in the earth," but it might also be rendered as "go to hell") more directly appropriate to its intended target. I must have been about eleven or twelve at the time, and full of wartime patriotic fervor, but, understanding enough by then not to argue with her, I confined myself to explaining what her sudden explosion of wrath showed that she had already intuited—that the figure of Uncle Sam was a stand-in for America.

Whenever I have told this story, I have been asked in wonderment how it was that my grandmother should have felt so little stake in the American war against the Nazis who in the very part of the world from which she stemmed were murdering Jews like herself, including actual relatives of her own. Why on earth should her fury have been directed not against Hitler but against "Uncle Sam"?

The answer is that so beaten-down and withdrawn was this stooped and wizened old woman with the face of a thousand wrinkles (who, I now realize with a shock as I conjure up that face, was

---

*The temporary conquest of Galicia was the only victory the Czarist army achieved in the First World War before being driven back, triggering a series of events that opened the way for the Bolshevik takeover of Russia in 1917.

then only in her early sixties, younger than I am now), and so exclusively preoccupied was she with her private troubles and woes, that it is entirely possible she knew nothing about the war and its connection with the fate of the Jews of Europe. For unlike my other grandmother, Runyeh, who avidly followed the serialized novels in the Yiddish papers every day, Esther Malkah was barely, if at all, literate.

But even if she did know more or less what was going on, she was altogether incapable of minding anyone's business but her own, which extended to her children and grandchildren and not a micromillimeter farther than that. Compared to their welfare, nothing was of any importance; and anything that harmed them (a category that self-evidently included being drafted into the army) was bad, period, with no discussion or elaboration needed or even allowed.

So it was that this piteous creature, who could be ignorant of, or perhaps even indifferent to, what was happening to the Jewish people among whom she had been born and then grown up and lived, was the same woman who some years later got herself killed by not hesitating an instant in chasing her two-year-old granddaughter, my cousin Sharon, into the street and throwing her own body between the child and an approaching automobile.

Flashing back now to the main point I was about to make when I so rudely interrupted myself: because my grandmothers (like my grandfathers) never learned much English, and because the two of them spent so much time with us as a result of their unhappy marriages, just about all the talking done at home throughout my childhood (including by me, a nonstop talker even then) had to be conducted in Yiddish.

Yiddish was, of course, the native language of Jews in the *shtetlakh*—the small towns and tiny villages—of Russia (and its domains), Poland, Rumania, and Hungary from which they had all emigrated to America. Galicia (*Galitzia* in Yiddish), the particular place from which, as I have indicated, my family came, was a province that could be described as being located in Southeast Poland or Western Ukraine, depending upon the political circumstances of a given period. To complicate matters even further, when my father left in 1912, it was with an Austrian passport, Galicia then still being part of the soon-to-be-defunct Hapsburg empire, with its capital called Lemberg. By 1920, when my mother left, the Treaty of Versailles had awarded Galicia to Poland, and the name of the capital had been changed to Lwow. When the Soviet Union ruled that part of the world between 1939 and 1989, it remained Lwow. But since the same province reverted to the newly independent Ukraine that emerged from the breakup of the Soviet empire, Lwow has become Lviv.

In terms of their national origins, then, my people were similar to a Jew I once knew from a town on the border between Hungary and Rumania. When asked what country he hailed from, he would reply that it was an impossible question to answer: on one day the residents of his town might be citizens or subjects of one state, and then on the next of another, while all the while neither they nor the town itself ever moved even an inch in one direction or another. "My town," he would grin, "was a miracle: it always migrated while staying in the same place."

Jews from other parts of East Europe like Russia proper, Lithuania, and northern Poland, and even more so from Germany, looked down upon the *Galitzianer* as backward ignoramuses and ne'er-do-wells—the hillbillies, as it were, of the Jewish people. There was a particle of truth to this accusation which it would carry me too far afield to explore. But this tiny particle was overwhelmed by and smothered in so much bigotry that to this day it comes as a surprise to certain people when I inform them that rabbinical sages existed in Galicia who were the equals in learning of their counterparts in the talmudic academies of Vilna[8] (which modestly styled itself "the Jerusalem of Lithuania"). Even more surprising is the revelation that the *Haskalah*, the Jewish Enlightenment—the movement that carried the Jews into the modern age, as an analogous one had earlier done for Western Christendom—had roots among intellectuals in Galicia (itself a concept that to believers in the stereotype sounds like an oxymoron) at least as deep as those in any other part of the East European Jewish world.

But perhaps the single bit of knowledge about Galicia that evokes the greatest amazement and/or amusement is that the author of the once notorious novel *Venus in Furs*, Count Leopold von Sacher-Masoch, from whose name the term "masochism" derives, came from and lived there.* To be sure, Sacher-Masoch was an Austrian nobleman, not a Jew. Yet he was a fervent philo-Semite who (when he was not concocting fantasies of being tormented by a dominatrix) wrote tender and loving sketches about the very Galician Jews who were so despised by their own coreligionists elsewhere.† But then, the minute anyone still in thrall to the negative stereotype of the *Galitzianer* hears this, astonishment gives way to wisecracks. On second thought, comes the retort, it figures that the father of masochism, and an aristocrat at that, would, if only through a subtle literary gesture, have abased himself before the lowly Jews of Galicia. Or: if Sacher-Masoch had lived in Berlin, he would probably have found no psychic profit in admiring the Jews there, who were too civilized to suit his purposes of self-abasement. Or: if his obverse, the Marquis de Sade, had been a native of Galicia rather than of France, his imagination would

---

*So, too, though born in the next century and located at the opposite end of the spectrum running from vice to virtue, did Karol Wojtyla, who would grow up to become Pope John Paul II.

†This friendly attitude toward Jews may be the only thing besides Galician roots that Sacher-Masoch had in common with Karol Wojtyla.

probably have gone to even greater lengths of cruelty in contemplating the Jews around him. And so on.

The accent in which the *Galitzianer* spoke Yiddish was broader than the one used by the Polish Jews to their north, and much different from the one that identified Jews in the territories ruled by the Czar of Russia, especially Lithuania ("*Litta*"), which, though much closer to the Russian than to the *Galitzianer* accent, had a distinctive sound of its own. These Russians and *Litvaks* and Poles far outnumbered the *Galitzianer* among the Jewish immigrants to the United States between the 1880s and the early 1920s (when the previously wide-open doors were slammed shut until the 1960s). Being in a majority, they had the power to make fun of the *Galitzianer* accent as yet another element of that group's alleged inferiority, even though none of the many accents in which Yiddish was spoken throughout Eastern Europe had any authoritative claim to greater correctness or cultivation than any other.

In any event, when I was a little boy, I spoke Yiddish—naturally like a real *Galitzianer*—as fluently as I did English. Furthermore, my English was so marked by a Yiddish accent that I was often mistaken for a recently arrived immigrant. Thus, when I was playing on the street with my friends, with whom I used English, grownup passersby would ask each other (in Yiddish), "Who is that little greenhorn?" To which I would respond with a combination of embarrassment and indignation.

This accent created a problem when at the age of five I was sent to the local public school, P.S. 28 (the very one that more than thirty years later, in 1967, would become the center of a great and highly portentous dispute between black radicals favoring "community control" and the largely Jewish United Federation of Teachers).

My memory of the incident is naturally dim. But it is clear enough to confirm the general accuracy of another favorite family tale, this one about a teacher who came upon me climbing alone up a staircase, apparently lost and in search of my class which had peeled off in some other direction while I was distractedly looking elsewhere. "Where are you going, little boy?" this teacher asked. "I goink op de stez," I am reputed to have replied. At this, the teacher instantly marched me off to the principal's office and had me placed in a remedial-speech class.

Obviously I could not have known such details at the time, but this teacher, like most of her colleagues, was a middle-aged Catholic woman of Irish ethnicity and (in the lingo of those days) an "old maid." Probably representing a majority of the teachers in the elementary division of the New York City public-school system of the 1930s, they were something like (and may even have seen themselves as) secular nuns. Be that as it may, they took their duties no less seriously than they would have done had they been wearing full habits and teaching in Catholic parochial schools. Of course, the most important of these duties was to make sure that their pupils learned how to read, write, and compute. But they had other solemn responsibilities as well, stemming from the special composition of the kids who had been put in their charge. This was the very height of the age of the "melting pot," and one of the main jobs of our teachers was to throw us into it and heat it up to as high a temperature as it might take to burn out our foreign impurities and turn us into real Americans.

That practically all of us had been born in America was of no account, since we were still marked by the habits and ways and mores of our immigrant parents at home. About a third of the student population of P.S. 28 was, like me, the offspring of Jews from tiny villages in East Europe; another third was made up of the children of immigrants from Sicily or Naples (who mostly spoke Italian at home, just as I did Yiddish); and the rest were Negroes whose parents, though not precisely immigrants, had recently come from the rural South and were just as foreign to the ways of the big city as the Jews and Italians. This being the Great Depression, we had one other thing in common: we were all dirt poor.

Not all our fathers were unemployed, though. My own, for instance, had a job as a milkman with a big company called Sheffield Farms, which meant that he drove all night long with a horse and wagon delivering orders to the stoops of broken-down old private houses and the doors of apartment buildings (that is, tenements). Like many of his generation who had been raised in extremely religious Orthodox households, he had gradually ceased observing more and more of the commandments that it would once have been unimaginable—and in Europe impossible—to violate, including the prohibition of work on the Sabbath. As outrageous as this was in the eyes of his parents, it was fortunate for his wife and two children. For the precious job he had managed to find in a time of mass unemployment required working on Saturday, and he would therefore have been unable to hold it if he had remained Orthodox. Not remaining Orthodox, however, did not entail joining either of the other two branches of American Judaism and becoming Conservative or Reform: the synagogue he did not attend, except on the High Holidays and other special occasions, was Orthodox; and in his own eyes, he was now a bad Jew (something like the Jewish equivalent of a lapsed Catholic).

As a milkman during the Depression, my father earned somewhere between two and three thousand dollars a year, which was the most he was ever to make in his entire life, including in the postwar age of affluence. This explains why—and it is only one of the multitudinous sociological oddities of my background that it took me ages to discover were not normal—my mother looked back on the Depression as a good rather than a bad time. For one thing, she was spared the shame that almost all of her neighbors had to suffer of being "on relief"—a shame that was not lessened by the fact that so many others were in the same boat through no fault of their own. Furthermore, prices were so low in the 1930s that even wages as minimal as my father's could buy a lot of groceries. The downside of these circumstances was that we always had relatives living with us either for free or for a pittance that theoretically covered their room and board. Thus, following my grandmother Runyeh's departure, a cousin and then an uncle moved in, each of whom in turn shared a bed with me and complained vociferously about how I always kicked them in my sleep.

The same economic oddity—reinforced by my mother's vivacity and hospitable nature—also accounts for the full house of aunts, uncles, and cousins who visited us every Sunday from the Lower East Side, distant neighborhoods in Brooklyn, and even the much farther-away Bronx. Such journeys could take an hour or even two in each direction, depending upon the number of transfers from subway to bus or trolley that might be required; but, nothing deterred, they kept coming without letup or surcease, gorging themselves on my mother's cooking and baking, playing pinochle, and consuming endless gallons of coffee and/or tea (drunk in a glass with lemon). "Those days," my mother—possibly the only person in America who looked back upon the Great Depression fondly—would say in future years when my father was still earning a pittance as compared with almost everyone else around her, "In those days, I was a queen! A queen!"

Among the neighbors "on relief" over whom her imagination reigned was one of her own younger sisters, who lived in an even smaller apartment in the same building as we. As grim and stingy as my mother was lively and generous, Gertie (or Khaya-Gittl) finally achieved release from the disgrace of being on the dole when her husband Hymie's younger brother wangled him a job on the loading platform of a small dairy owned by a friend. I never knew whether the cases of milk my uncle Hymie would bring home with him every day had been pilfered or were a perk of the job. But, acquired by fair means or foul, they were used by Gertie to go into business for herself. Her "route" consisted almost entirely of nearby relatives whom she bullied into buying from her instead of going to the grocery store or getting deliveries from big companies like the one my father worked for.

Having received her merchandise for free, Gertie might have been expected to sell it at bargain rates, especially to my mother* and her other siblings. But such a thing was not in Gertie's nature. She regarded it as axiomatic that her prices should be exactly the same as those that were charged by the stores or the milkmen, giving her a profit of one-hundred percent (minus the work her husband put into *shlepping* the goods home and the labor she added in delivering them to her customers).

So scrupulous was she in following this pricing practice (her own home-made version of the Marxist theory of the surplus value of labor, of which she could never have heard) that one day, when the major dairies announced a rise in the price of milk, Gertie informed her customers that she was no longer charging ten cents, or however much it was, a bottle. When they asked her why, she solemnly replied, "Because milk just went up a penny." Out of a combination of the pity they all for some obscure reason felt toward her, together with the fear of provoking the righteous wrath that, having gently tried to bargain her down in the first place, they knew was sure to erupt if they rejected this demented demand, everyone, including my mother, went along.

Gertie and Hymie had a son, Raphael (called Rafie), who was exactly a year older than I, and though we actually took a dislike to each other almost from birth, we were constantly thrown together because our two families lived in the same apartment building. We were also forced by our mothers into a never-ending rivalry in school. Everything he accomplished I was expected to equal or (God should only be so good to my mother) surpass in the following year. Unfortunately, the competition got off to a bad start from my mother's point of view because *he* had not been assigned to a

---

*I should explain that my father's "route" was in a different neighborhood, and so we were not his customers. Nor did Sheffield give him a price break on milk, let alone let him have it for free.

remedial-speech class—whatever that might be; and whatever it was, certainly it could not be interpreted as a badge of honor—upon entering first grade. Neither had any such disturbing thing happened to my sister five years earlier.

In the age of multiculturalism that dawned on America a half-century later, any teacher doing to a black or Latino or Asian kid what that teacher did to me would (I exaggerate only slightly) have been surrounded in a trice by federal marshals materializing out of the very walls of the school, arrested for attempted cultural genocide, read her Miranda rights, and carted off in handcuffs to the applause of the child's parents and sundry liberal spokesmen. But luckily for me, neither my parents nor those of any of my contemporaries would ever have dreamed of questioning the right of the school to conduct itself as it saw fit, either in this or in any other matter.

They did not, for instance, take offense when their children were inspected every morning for clean hands and fingernails and teeth. They did not rise up in anger at the clear implication that when a child of theirs received a demerit for some deficiency of personal hygiene, this was a reflection on them and an adverse judgment on their parental competence. They did not storm into the principal's office protesting that their ancestral cultures had a different attitude toward things of this kind (which was in fact true of all three groups in my school).

Nor (shifting now to another sensitive area) did the Jews among them object to the hymn their children sang every morning in assembly: "Holy! Holy! Holy! Lord God Almighty! / Early in the morning our song shall rise to Thee: / Holy, Holy, Holy! Merciful and Mighty! / God in Three Persons, Blessed Trinity." When, already well into adulthood, I heard this hymn being sung somewhere and it dawned on me for the first time what the words signified, I burst out laughing at the thought of the furies that would now have been unleashed on P.S. 28 by the American Civil Liberties Union and Jewish defense organizations like the Anti-Defamation League and the American Jewish Congress. They would have condemned the singing of any hymn, even one drawn from the Hebrew Bible, as an egregious violation of the separation of church and state, and they would have regarded a blatantly Christian hymn like "Holy, Holy, Holy" as an especially aggressive act of religious discrimination against the Jewish children to boot. In the 1930s, however, the First Amendment was not yet interpreted by the courts as prohibiting prayer in the public schools. And besides, I would bet that the Irish-Catholic ladies who chose "Holy, Holy, Holy" and who knew next to nothing about the Jewish religion or its relation to Christianity, innocently thought that it was nonsectarian because it contained no explicit mention of Jesus.

What added to the comedy and also the poignancy of the situation was that neither we children nor our parents (who heard us sing the hymn on special ceremonial occasions to which they would be invited and which they would respectfully attend) had the foggiest notion of what we would have been affirming and celebrating had we understood the words. Moreover, even if they had, I doubt that they would have had the nerve to object any more than they did to the daily inspection of their children for proper habits of personal hygiene. The authority of the school was absolute so far as they were concerned; and they humbly accepted, and indeed were grateful for, the efforts it made not only to educate their children but to Americanize them as well.*

It was, by the way, this experience of hymn-singing in P.S. 28 that turned me into a bemused skeptic when—in one of the central battles of the "culture wars" that would be unleashed in the

---

*I was astonished to learn from an essay by John O'Sullivan in *National Review* that even in the city of Liverpool, England, and as late as the 1950s, the same fin-

subsequent decades—the issue of prayer in the schools heated up. So far as I could tell on the basis of my own experience, both the proponents and the opponents wildly exaggerated the effects of either permitting or prohibiting the kids to engage in religious exercises of whatever kind during school hours.

Of course, I had no problem understanding the *symbolic* importance of this issue, in connection with the battle over the role of religion in American life and its claim to a place in what Father Richard J. Neuhaus dubbed "the public square." I also understood that Jews who lived not in New York but in parts of the country where they were a small minority surrounded by Gentiles felt threatened, and inevitably discriminated against, by any infringement on the religious neutrality of the schools their children attended: they knew from their own experience that any such infringement was bound to have a Christian flavor.

Still, it seemed a bit bizarre to me that these fears should have been exacerbated rather than relieved by the decline from the late 1940s onward of anti-Semitism in America.* But now that Christians were less eager to persecute them than to marry their sons and daughters (as my friend, the social critic and editor Irving Kristol, observed in one of his justly celebrated quips), Jews suddenly began realizing that there were benign as well as evil ways through which their own survival as a distinct people could be endangered. It was out of this worry that the issue of "Jewish continuity" was destined to be born in the 1990s and to grow into almost as great a preoccupation of the American Jewish commu-

---

gernail inspection was conducted. It would appear that children like himself, who had Irish names (though his mother actually was English), were no more assumed by their teachers in England to have been taught how to look after their own persons than we Jews, Italians, and Negroes were in the America of the 1930s (ironically by teachers whose own roots were in Ireland), and were therefore thought to need help if they were to become properly Anglicized.

*This decline is discussed at length below, in Part Three.

nity as Israel had been since that country's physical survival had come under direct military assault in 1967.

But all that was still in the far historical distance when I was assigned to the remedial-speech class in P.S. 28. I was only five or possibly six years old then, and I remember very little about it. What I do remember is that I sat for a semester (or was it a whole year?) with kids who had other and more serious kinds of defects than a foreign accent that needed to be corrected, such as stuttering, lisping, and trouble with "s" or "l." No matter: we were all put repeatedly through the same exercises, which were designed to condition us into placing the tongue and shaping the mouth so as to make all the consonants and vowels come out sounding right.

Apparently the end result was to eradicate all traces of my Yiddish accent but without putting a Brooklyn accent in its place. How this came about is still an enigma to me, considering that even most of my teachers spoke Brooklynese (recognizable not from the "dese" and "dose" of showbiz caricature but from the pronunciation of certain vowels). So, for that matter, did all my friends and schoolmates, except the Negroes, every one of whom had a Southern accent. Was it racism that kept *them* out of the remedial-speech class, or did the peculiar prejudices of the day regard a Southern accent as more acceptable than a foreign one like mine?

I cannot answer that question with any greater confidence than I can comprehend how I emerged from remedial-speech training sounding more like an announcer on one of the "coast-to-coast" radio programs of the 1930s than like a kid from a Brooklyn slum. (Most of these announcers affected a kind of neutral English, purged of any regional flavor, presumably to avoid putting off potential listeners from this part of the country or that.) My best guess is that the remedial-speech teachers of the period had been trained to aim at precisely such neutrality, and that they succeeded with me, a prize pupil if there ever was one, whose report cards from the early grades on up fully compensated my parents for whatever shame they may have felt when I had been singled out for my inability to speak properly. I even surpassed my cousin Rafie academically as we went along, though he would eventually fulfill the highest ambition of his own parents (an ambition common to their entire generation) by becoming a doctor.*

I ,alas, grew up to become something that my poor mother would never quite be able to define or to measure against the various forms of professional or commercial achievement with which she was familiar. A petite and very pretty woman of high-voltage vitality, charm, and cleverness, as well as the best story-teller (and, to violate another stereotype, the best poker player) I have ever run into, she would invariably become the immediate center of attention in any group in which she might find herself—even a hospital ward. But there was some deep timidity in her nature that kept her from venturing outside her own milieu, either physically or intellectually. Rarely did she leave Jewish Brooklyn for any purpose other than to visit a relative in the Bronx or—in later years—in Florida. The only people outside her own extended family of whom she was not fearful, or in whom she could take an interest, were people like herself: Jews from East Europe who, even after spending far more of their lives in America than in the towns where they were born, remained more comfortable communicating with one another in Yiddish than in English.

---

*Both the high prestige of the medical profession among Jews from East Europe in those days and the bragging it invariably bred are summed up in the classic joke about the mother running up and down the beach crying: "Help! Help! My son, the chief of surgery at Mt. Sinai, is drowning!"

But she did more than accept whole hog the assumptions and attitudes of that milieu; she even held on tenaciously to the ideas and valuations of her childhood. Never in her whole life would she stop insisting, for example, that a certain uncle of hers "back home" (as, even after reaching her nineties, she always thought of *Galitzia*, which she had left at the age of seventeen) was "very rich." It made no difference that she had by now seen enough in America—even if much of it was on television—to have realized that this was only a little girl's stringently limited impression; she simply would not surrender any of the inner baggage she had carried with her from "home."

My father had no comparable difficulty, none whatsoever, in understanding who and what I had become, and—out of the deeply repressed aspirations he had no doubt once entertained for himself—was very proud that his son had grown up to be an intellectual, an editor, and a literary man rather than a doctor or a lawyer or a businessman. But out of a sickly combination of reticence, snobbery, and the self-hatred from which he suffered over his own sense of himself as a failure, he would never deign to explain any of it to my mother (or anyone else): if they were so stupid and ignorant, they deserved only contempt, and that was what he gave them. Even my mother, whom I feel sure he loved, was at the receiving end of this sneering attitude of his, especially when it came to me and my career. Consequently she had a great deal of trouble competing in the bragging-about-their-sons game that was the main recreational activity of the old crones among whom she would live in the twenty-five years remaining to her following his death in 1971 at the age of seventy-five. (She herself died at ninety-three.)

"So what is he? A joinalist?" they would demand of her as she vainly tried to describe the difference between a journalist and a writer for magazines of which no one had ever heard, but which I had assured her were far superior to the likes of *The Reader's Digest*. Nor could she ever impress these ferocious women enough to satisfy her when she told them that I was even the editor of such a magazine, especially as the pay was nothing to write home about when compared with what they, often lying by a large factor, alleged their own sons were earning.

Tragically, I could not even measure up economically to the dentists among these sons. True, in all their eyes, dentists were, and always would be, failed doctors. Yet once their dentist sons began making a great deal of money and buying grand houses out on Long Island or (more rarely) up in Westchester to which they dutifully chauffeured their mothers every weekend in the fancy cars they owned (and woe betide them if they had to skip one of these visits), the bitter disappointment of that long-ago rejection from medical school faded. Not so completely, however, that it could not instantly be reawakened by an unlucky encounter with the mother of a doctor, who could trump them every time, including on the all-important question of which son made more money.

Still, I became what I became, and I believe there was a connection between where I landed professionally and what happened to me in that remedial-speech class. I am of course well aware that foreign accents did not prevent Henry Kissinger or Zbigniew Brzezinski, and countless academic eminences, from achieving high positions in American government and society. I know, too, that other very distinguished careers in other fields were also made by people with accents reeking of the lower classes of New York. Yet I cannot help feeling that my own life would have been very different if I had never been forced to speak like a classier and more cultivated person than I actually was.

Nothing, for instance, will ever persuade me that I would have won the scholarships I later did to Columbia and Cambridge Universities if even a residual trace had remained in my speech of the little boy who told a teacher that he was "goink op de stez" when he was going up the stairs. Yes, I had the grades and the recommendations. But in 1946, when I was graduated from high school, enough snobbery (not always easily distinguishable from an old-fashioned species of genteel anti-Semitism) still existed in America to have worked against a teenage version of that little boy who retained his childhood accent even in an attenuated form. He might easily have seemed unfit for promotion into a higher rank of society in the minds of at least some of the people by whom I was either sponsored or interviewed.

Almost certainly, Harriet Haft, the high-school teacher I called "Mrs. K." when I came to write about her two decades later in my book *Making It*, would have been prevented by her fierce class-consciousness from developing as intense an interest in me as she did; and in the absence of that interest, it might well never have occurred to me that I could attend an Ivy League college. Mrs. Haft had her heart set on Harvard, to which I did in fact win a scholarship, but since it covered only tuition, the only way I could afford to take it would involve working long hours to pay for my room and board. Instead I happily and gratefully chose the scholarship I was also offered to Columbia, which would pay my tuition and a modest stipend as well, while allowing me to live at home, where there was no problem of room and board.

But it is not this order of sociological factors alone—the ones I concentrated on in *Making It*—that I have in mind when I stress the importance of the remedial-speech class I was forced to attend. I am even tempted to go so far as to say that, without it, I might not have wound up practicing a profession that gave my mother so much trouble understanding, assessing, and boasting about, but that gave me so much pleasure and even greater satisfaction.

I suppose it is a bit of a stretch to claim that I would never have come to love poetry if that class had not made my ear so sensitive to the sound of the English language. But it probably is true that this love would not have shown itself as early as it did. And it is no stretch at all to draw a direct line from the training I received as a little boy to my later emergence as an amateur or low-rent Henry Higgins. Thus, during my two-year hitch in the army (1953–55), I would win bets by guessing from their accents where my barracks mates had come from. Sometimes it was easy: only someone completely deaf would be incapable of distinguishing a Boston from a Minneapolis accent. But I could do better than that. Usually, I could hear the subtle differences between, say, Boston and Providence, or Wisconsin and Minnesota, or Trenton and Philadelphia. And at my very best, I could even tell from the mixture of his accents that a particular person had lived in two or three different places at various times in his life.

This talent, if that is what it was, has by now largely gone the way of the prodigiously retentive memory that reinforced it—I once had trouble forgetting things, not, as now, remembering them—and the dimming of other mental faculties to which the septuagenarian mind is more often than not heir. So, too, with poetry, which I have long since given up writing and which I have even stopped reading with any regularity.

As to the writing: it started when I was about seven or eight, but the training of my ear was not the only push that propelled me into trying my hand at it. A mighty incentive was also introduced into the picture when my older sister was persuaded by our parents to take what was then known as a "commercial" rather than an "academic" course in high school. This meant that, upon graduation, she would not be qualified to apply to college (although she certainly had the brains for it and had always done very well in school). She would, however, be equipped with the skills, principally shorthand and typing, to get a job as a secretary.

The main reason Millie was pressured into going this route had to do with the insecurities instilled in our parents by the Great Depression of the 1930s; and besides, as a girl, and a very pretty one at that, what need had she of college when she would in all likelihood get married in short order? Which, as it turned out, she did, having met her husband Solomon Zuckerman when she went to work for six dollars a week as a secretary in the store-front office in Brooklyn he shared with another lawyer. It was a happy marriage that produced two children, Alan and Evan, who went on to have two children each of their own, and it lasted fifty-five years until Sol's death in 1999. She herself, after her kids were both in school, went back to work, and in due course she would achieve a good deal of power as the assistant to one president of the New York City Council after another.

For me, if not for her (as she would come to feel in spite of how well things turned out), Millie's commercial course proved to be an unexpected boon. Because at first she had trouble learning how to touch-type (she would eventually do so at the speed of champions), the grave decision was made after much discussion and calculation around our kitchen table that she must be provided with a machine at home on which to practice. And so, with the help of an installment plan to pay for it, into our house came a black Smith-Corona portable, which sat in its matching black case on a dark brown metal typing table featuring a fold-up side panel to hold material for copying.

I was enchanted with this machine, which surpassed any toy I had ever owned or even seen, and there was no keeping me away from it. Neither stern exhortations nor angry reproaches nor threats of punishment could hold me back. Locking the case did not solve the problem, either, since I always managed to find the key when no one was looking. Finally, my parents surrendered to the inevitable. The only way to prevent me from doing damage to this precious and, for them, enormously expensive, piece of equipment, was for my sister to teach me how to use it properly.

She hated having to do so, especially as to her it seemed yet another mark of the greater favor in which our parents held me, as the baby of the family, as a boy, and as a student whose teachers—always on the lookout for the urban equivalent of flowers blushing unseen in the desert air—were already beginning to tell them was something special.* Like all Jewish parents, mine would have died before admitting they did not love each of their children "the same," and in some deep sense this was true. But there was plenty of reason for my sister to have her doubts.

Still, being a most obedient girl, Millie had no choice but to teach me how to use the precious Smith-Corona. And so at a very early age I became a very good and a very fast typist. Yet once I had mastered this skill through the diligent, and indeed obsessive, practice of the exercises involved in learning the keyboard and becoming adept at racing around it without looking, I grew bored with what now seemed meaningless mechanical activity. I would try to relieve my boredom by copying pieces out of the newspaper, but soon enough I started writing things of my own: mostly poems, but also stories.

Fortunately, none of this juvenilia has survived, and so I can only guess at what it was like. The poems must have been imitations of jingly things like Joyce Kilmer's "Trees" (which begins with the lines: "I think that I shall never see / A poem lovely as a tree" and ends: "Poems are made by fools like me, / But only God can make a tree"). "Trees," I believe, was taught to children in the early grades in those years. I thought it was wonderful. The senti-

---

*The image of flowers blushing unseen in the desert comes, of course, from a once very popular English poem, later to become one of my own favorites: Thomas Gray's "Elegy Written in a Country Churchyard" (1750). If I am not mistaken (and I hope I am), it is now almost completely forgotten, at least in America, though I would still rank it among the greatest written in the eighteenth century. Gray, strolling through a little cemetery in which only poor people are buried, laments all the talent he imagines has been lost in that social class for lack of the necessary nurture. "Some mute inglorious Milton here may lie," he writes, for "Full many a gem of purest ray serene / The dark unfathom'd caves of ocean bear: / Full many a flower was born to blush unseen, / And waste its sweetness on the desert air."

ment was sublime, but the sound of the verse and the rhymes was even better (in fact, it had been set to music and was much loved at some point as a song).

Nor did it hurt that Kilmer was such a romantic figure, having been killed at an early age in the First World War as a member of the Fighting 69th. In the film made in 1940 about that fabled regiment, a minor movie star, Jeffrey Lynn, played Kilmer, and in one scene (I would swear to this, though my memory may be deceiving me after sixty years) he was shown marching with the words of a poem running through his head. They stuck in *my* head as "Boots—boots—boots—trampling up and down again! / There's no escape from the war." But just a minute ago, looking them up in *Bartlett's Familiar Quotations*, I was embarrassed to discover that they were written not by Joyce Kilmer in 1918 but by Rudyard Kipling in 1903, and that, moreover, I had them slightly wrong.* Perhaps it was not even in *The Fighting 69th* that I first came upon them; or perhaps the screenwriter either mistakenly attributed them to Kilmer or simply meant to have him shown quoting Kipling to himself rather than composing a poem of his own.

Even so, those misattributed and slightly misquoted lines still gave me an early inkling of what words could do and evoke, not only through what they signify but through their placement in rhythmic patterns and the use of their very sounds to reinforce and make the meaning more vivid and immediate. I could hear in the harsh spondees (a word I had not yet learned) the endlessly stomping boots, and this then propelled me into an intimation of the endlessness of the war and the inescapable doom it promised.

---

*The correct version is "Boots—boots—boots—boots—movin' up and down again! / There's no discharge in the war!" I had only three repetitions of "boots" and I did not know that the second line, which I also got slightly wrong, is lifted from the biblical book of Ecclesiastes.

I have always thought that some people are born with an exceptionally good ear, and that I was one of them (which did not mean that it could not be made better, as mine was, through training). I also think that this is an inherited trait—a belief that has been confirmed by my own children, one of whom, John, is an extraordinary mimic and another of whom, his older sister Ruth Blum, picked up Spanish as a kid on the streets of the Upper West Side of Manhattan, where we lived for twenty-odd years, and could speak it in all three of the accents of her friends' parents (Cuban, Puerto Rican, and Dominican). Moving to Israel when she was already about twenty, and knowing very little Hebrew, Ruthie was soon chattering merrily away like a native, and no one ever believed she had only just come from America. But there is no need to stick to my own children for confirmation, when it is common knowledge that musical talent, which depends on a good ear even more than does poetry, runs in families.

Having mentioned music, I find that I am once more unable to turn aside the temptation of a digression—this time to reveal another curiously untypical detail about my life. It is that I may well be the only boy in the relatively recent history of the Jewish people who was not only spared the pressure to take up an instrument (usually the violin) but who begged for lessons and was refused. Many excuses were given: we couldn't afford it; my father, who slept during the day after working all night, would be disturbed when I practiced; and anyway, no one else on either side of our huge extended family took music lessons (here, I ruefully admit, was one of the elements of truth in the negative stereotype of the *Galitzianer*).

The only acquaintance I had with classical music therefore came through a music-appreciation program in school that consisted of a teacher playing snippets of the main themes from famous pieces on the piano and providing mnemonic devices to help us remember what they were ("This is the symphony," we would sing to its opening bars, "that Schubert wrote but never finished"; or "Barcarolle from *Tales of Hoffmann* written by Offenbach"—and so on). There was a contest at the end of the program and I won it, receiving a little medallion shaped like a harp that could be screwed into my belt. But that was the end of any musical training I was to receive, and it was many years before I would overcome a resistance to classical music and learn how to listen to it (at which point I became, and still am, an addict of almost unhealthy proportions).

Resistance to classical music was almost universal in my circle of friends, all of whom were, in my grandfather M'shitzik's unshakable estimation, *konnabums*. This was his transposition into Yiddish of "corner bums," meaning boys who hung out, as Brooklyn kids always did, around the candy store that was located on just about every corner of the borough, and who he assumed (not altogether inaccurately, except on the issue of whistling) were always up to no good. Like every other *konnabum*, I jeered at classical music as something foreign: anyone with a taste for it was unmanly and possibly even a "fag."

Popular music, however, was perfectly acceptable, and one was permitted to be mad for it, which I definitely was. I followed the great swing bands and the vocalists of the period with as much avidity as I did the baseball teams; and just as I knew the batting averages of practically every player in the major leagues, so I could easily sing the words of almost every popular song around, and most of the old ones too. A contrarian even then, I liked Harry James better than Glenn Miller (which somehow went with rooting for the rough and not always reliable Brooklyn Dodgers rather than the always smooth and perfect New York Yankees). I also thought that Dick Haymes, not Frank Sinatra, should have won the great "Battle of the Baritones" staged by one of our local radio stations,* and (again showing bad judgment) I considered Artie Shaw a greater clarinetist than Benny Goodman. Then, as I grew a little older, I also got interested in bands like Stan Kenton's and singers like Ella Fitzgerald, Anita O'Day, and Mel Tormé, who bridged the gap between swing and jazz (though I never did cotton to the "progressive" jazz of Dizzy Gillespie and Charlie Parker).

But it is the music produced by words—and specifically the words of the English language—not the music coming out of notes and instruments, with which I am concerned here, and to which I must now return. And I want to do so by way of picking up on the speculation that even if I was born with a good ear, the re-medial-speech class helped make it more sensitive. I was put in that class in order to correct what was considered a stigma and an obstacle to the process of Americanization, which the elementary-school teachers of that era were as much expected to further as they were to make us literate and numerate. In all this they suc-ceeded brilliantly with me. But little did they know that, while rid-ding this child of immigrants of his foreign accent, they were—by making him preternaturally conscious at so early an age of the way words sounded—simultaneously presenting him with the serendip-itous gift of a key to the inexhaustibly rich treasure-house of liter-ature in the English language.

Using this key, and a public-library card, I became a great reader from the start. Not that everything I read was English or American in origin. Andrew Lang's series of fairy-tale collec-tions—*The Blue Fairy Book*, *The Red Fairy Book*, and so on—had been written by a Scot in English, but the Grimms' fairy tales,

---

*Adding to the resonances here, Haymes was briefly married to the movie star I considered the sexiest of all, Rita Hayworth, and then Sinatra captured Ava Gard-ner, who ran her a very close second.

which I loved just as much, were translations from the German. The volumes of mythology I also adored were all translated from other languages. My contrarian nature manifesting itself in this department, too, I liked the Norse myths better than the Greek or their Roman versions. Yet—and again I give credit to the training I received in that remedial-speech class—I was almost abnormally alive to the language of these books. The euphonious style of Lang was as mesmerizing as the stories he told, and I was also captivated by the way with words of the writers who had been translated from foreign originals (though I doubt that I realized then that these *were* translations).

As time went on, I discovered fiction, and gnawed my way like a termite through the children's section of the library devoted to it. I devoured the thrilling sports novels of John R. Tunis and the adventure novels of Rafael Sabatini, and countless others by authors whose names I have ungratefully forgotten. And then I came upon Mark Twain—not in the library but at home. This was unusual, since we owned very few books, and most of those were in Hebrew or Yiddish. But whether as a premium for buying something else, possibly the encyclopedia we also owned, or through a special cut-rate subscription offer from one of those door-to-door salesmen who were so common during the Great Depression, my parents acquired a set of the complete works of Mark Twain, bound in pale yellow covers. These I promptly seized upon, and though a few were too difficult for me at first, I loved *The Adventures of Tom Sawyer* (which, by the way, is much harder from the point of view of vocabulary than boys' books later became, as I would discover when reading it to my own young children). But I am proud to say that as a kid I was already a good enough literary critic to like *Adventures of Huckleberry Finn,** a much greater work, even more.

Sic: for some reason there is no *The* in the title, though Twain did use the definite article in the title of his book about Tom Sawyer.

Meanwhile, I steadily pounded poems out of the Smith-Corona portable, and the occasional story as well. However, it was not until junior high school (grades 7 through 9 under the system that then prevailed in New York, which in my case, because I had been skipped several times in elementary school, translated into the younger-than-usual ages of eleven to thirteen), that I began reading poetry—real poetry—in earnest. It was then that I got hold (a gift from my sister or my soon-to-be brother-in-law? or did I buy it for myself?) of a mass-paperback anthology entitled something like *100 Great American Poems*, all of which I read and reread and a good number of which I memorized in whole or in part (among them John Greeneaf Whittier's "Barbara Frietchie," Oliver Wendell Holmes's "Old Ironsides," Walt Whitman's "O Captain! My Captain!," Vachel Lindsay's "The Congo," and Edwin Arlington Robinson's "Miniver Cheevy").

Then in ninth grade I had my first taste of Shakespeare, when we were required to study *Julius Caesar*. I wish I could say I instantly recognized that it was in another league from the mostly second-rate stuff in my anthology. But in all truth it was tough going, and I did not begin to appreciate Shakespeare until I read his complete plays in chronological order in a most remarkable course I took at Columbia with a professor named Andrew Chiappe about four years later.

What I never found tough going at that stage of my development as a reader of poetry, nor needed any tutoring to appreciate (at least to some limited degree), was Whitman's *Leaves of Grass*. I cannot say where or how I first acquired the abridged copy of it that fell into my hands, but it intoxicated me from the first, and kept me in the same drunken state as I read it over and over and over again. Mercifully, I have no such vivid memory of the countless imitations that poured out of the Smith-Corona, but what does flood back into my mind is the astonishment I felt when I got to high school and was told in no uncertain terms that Whitman was not the right model for an aspiring young poet to follow.

The bearer of this information was the same Mrs. Haft who was bent on civilizing me, but whose conception of what that meant entailed more than instruction in manners and in how to dress. She was a WASP of patrician stock with a rich (and very assimilated) Jewish husband—not the kind of woman one would expect to find teaching English in a Brooklyn high school and acting as faculty adviser to its student newspaper, whose staff I joined as soon as I could. Nor would one expect a woman of her background and aggressively prissy manner to be as advanced, unconventional, and daring in her literary tastes as she turned out to be.

Yet there she was in Boys High, where I saw a lot of her after regular hours in the office of the student paper, *The Red and Black*, which took its name from the school colors and not from the title of Stendhal's novel. (Come to think of it, though, as a kid from Brooklyn who would wind up aspiring to and then living amid the glories and grandeurs of Manhattan, I had something in common with the hero of that novel, Julien Sorel, one of the quintessential embodiments of a type my future mentor and friend Lionel Trilling would later call "the young man from the provinces," who goes off to Paris and is then taken in hand and polished to the right degree of sheen by an older married woman.)

In her capacity as my English teacher, Mrs. Haft told me about T. S. Eliot, of whom I had never before heard. He was, she said, very difficult, but far superior to Whitman, and he was one of the modern poets I had to read and study if I was going to become one myself. But in the office of the paper after regular school hours, she would (though not before exacting solemn promises of secrecy) slip me improper poems like Robinson Jeffers's *The Roan Stallion*, highly erotic by prevailing standards, and Djuna Barnes's novel *Nightwood*, which dealt with the even more shocking subject of lesbianism (and came with a laudatory introduction by Eliot himself). She also presented me as a gift on my fifteenth birthday with a cardboard-bound but exquisitely produced little volume of selections from the poems of John Keats, on whom I was soon hooked, and complemented this perfectly proper offering with a naughty companion from the same series—a volume of Charles Baudelaire's *Flowers of Evil* in French (which, to her disgust, I had not chosen as one of the two foreign languages we were required to study, opting instead for Spanish and Latin) with English translations on facing pages.

Lest all this sound as though Mrs. Haft were trying to seduce me into a sexual affair, as was invariably the case with the older women who took up Julien Sorel and other young men from the provinces in other French novels (like Lucien de Rubempré in Balzac's *Lost Illusions*), I hasten to dispel any such impression. I never had an affair with Mrs. Haft, and if some of the books she gave me to read would in a later cultural climate be taken as gestures of seduction, there was not the slightest hint of it then.

But Mrs. Haft's intentions toward me were not only honorable; they were also more far-reaching than any sexual hanky-panky could ever have been. High-school teachers, unlike those in elementary school, did not have as a part of their duties the furthering of the process of Americanization that began with fingernail inspections in the first grade. Yet that is precisely what Mrs. Haft—wearing, as it were, her "Mrs. K." hat—had taken it upon herself to do with me in the area of manners and dress. More important in the present context, however, were her separate but complementary efforts to refine my literary sensibility—efforts that constituted a continuation of the correlative process that began with the remedial-speech training I was also given in the first grade. Because the foundation had been laid back then, she was able to build on it now; and build she did. Her long-range goal may have been to transform me into what I would one day designate a "facsimile WASP." But being a genuine lover of literature in touch with the latest developments (which was more than could be said of many, or perhaps even most, members of that class), she added a priceless item to the usual requirements for eligibility. Which is to say that she boosted me to the second level of my novitiate as a full-fledged American not only in the social but also in the cultural sense.

The third level was left for Columbia to help me climb. The four years I spent there, from 1946 to 1950, were extraordinary in a number of ways. First of all, because of the GI bill, which paid the tuition of soldiers who had just been discharged from the armed services, half or more of my classmates were veterans. This meant that, entering college at the age of sixteen, I was immediately thrown into the company of men who were anywhere from five to fifteen years older than I. A lot of them were already married, and having lost so much time to the war, they were in no mood for the frivolities that had once marked life in an Ivy League college like Columbia. They were in a hurry to get going, and they were intensely serious about their studies. It is unlikely that the Columbia campus had ever before been enveloped in so earnest an atmosphere, and I doubt that it ever was again.

Secondly, Columbia in those years probably had the best faculty of any undergraduate college anywhere. At Harvard, famous senior professors never, or only rarely, had any truck with undergraduates except perhaps to deliver lectures to hundreds of them with whom they had no personal contact; their actual teaching was confined to the supervision of graduate students working for advanced degrees. At Columbia, by contrast, most of the senior professors taught small classes, seminar-style, in the undergraduate college. Even as a freshman, then, one could find oneself being instructed by and getting to know the likes of eminent literary men like Lionel Trilling and Mark Van Doren, and highly distinguished classical scholars like Moses Hadas.

The reason this could happen had to do with the third extraordinary feature of Columbia, which was the two courses, then known as Humanities and Contemporary Civilization (or CC), that all freshmen and sophomores, no matter what they eventually intended to specialize in, were required to take. The purpose of these courses was to give the students a chance to become acquainted with the great classics of Western literature and philosophy. The selection of authors might vary from year to year (Rabelais, say, might be dropped and Dostoevsky added), but only within very narrow limits, since there was general agreement in the faculty as to the pool of works from which to draw.

The powerful effect of these courses was well described in a report issued in the late 1950s by the sociologist Daniel Bell, who claimed that they shocked many students into "a new appreciation of the dimensions of thought and feeling." I have at various times in the past vouched for the accuracy of that claim, and I do so again now. Before Columbia I had never truly understood what men were doing when they committed words to paper. Before Columbia I had never truly understood what an idea was or how the mind could play with it. Before Columbia, I had never truly understood that, as an American, I was the product of a tradition, that past ages had been inhabited by people like myself, and that the things they had done and the thoughts they had thought bore a direct relation to me and to the world in which I lived. At Columbia, through those two courses, all this began becoming clear to me, and I would never be the same again.

Curiously, there was next to nothing written by Americans in the vast reading lists of these courses, which began with the ancient Greeks and ended somewhere in the twentieth century. Nor, for that matter, was there much American literature on offer in the English department to anyone who might wish to study it. The vast majority of the authors taught in the English department were *English* (or, more precisely, considering the large number of Irishmen and Scots among them, British).

This in itself refutes the charge later hurled by the Left that curricula like the one at Columbia concealed an underlying political agenda shaped by the propagandistic imperatives of the cold war. Obviously, if patriotic indoctrination had been the objective, America would not have been scanted so drastically in favor of Europe. In any event, at Columbia, both courses long predated the cold war. Humanities had been designed in the 1930s, and from the start it reflected the belief that students ought to be introduced to the books that had shaped the world in which they lived. It was further assumed, in the spirit of the famous definition of criticism framed by the great Victorian literary critic Matthew Arnold, that these books contained the "best that has been known and thought in the world."

As for CC, it is true that it had originally been instituted with the open intention of demonstrating the greatness of their Western heritage to Columbia students. But that was in the 1920s, long before "the West" had come to be used as a term in opposition to the Communist world, and even longer before the idea of Western civilization had been turned into the kind of political issue it would become for radicals from the 1960s onward. The radicals began with a campaign to abolish Humanities and CC and courses like them in other colleges; they failed at Columbia but were relatively successful elsewhere. Then, after a long lull, this campaign started up again in the 1980s at Stanford.

After such a course had been reintroduced there, students led by Jesse Jackson and spokesmen of other minority groups, joined now by the feminists, marched around the campus shouting, "Hey hey, ho ho, Western Culture's got to go." They demanded that the course be dropped because the reading list—made up of the likes of Plato, St. Augustine, Dante, Galileo, Rousseau, Mill, and Nietzsche—was marked (in repulsive phrasing that had already become tiresomely familiar) by a "European-Western and male bias." Alternatively, the course could be kept, but only if it were subjected to affirmative action through the inclusion of (in another tiresomely familiar litany) "works by women, minorities, and persons of color."

. . .

I must admit that, coarse and vulgar though their language was, these people knew what they were doing. For in addition to shocking students into "a new appreciation of the dimensions of thought and feeling," something else had tended to happen through such courses as well. Bell characterized it as a kind of "conversion experience"—a conversion not to another religion but, "so to speak, to culture." Though he did not say so explicitly, by culture Bell specifically meant the heritage of Western civilization, and on this point too I have in the past and still can offer personal testimony that bears him out.

There is no doubt that Columbia left me with a reverence for Western civilization—and by extension for its great heir, defender, and new leader, America—that was nothing short of religious in intensity and that has remained alive all my life, including that part of it I spent in the camp of the radical Left. It was because they wanted to put a stop to this "conversion experience" that the radical students of the 1960s first zeroed in on the courses that were producing it. Beyond that, their aim was to clear the way for the opposite conversion experience: one that would leave most undergraduates feeling not reverence for Western civilization and/or America but hatred and contempt.

In other words, it was not, as the radicals claimed in their original assault, because the great books were "irrelevant" that they should no longer be studied; it was because they were all *too* relevant. Similar bad faith was shown in the complaint of the feminists and the students "of color" in the 1980s that they felt ignored and demeaned by not being prominently or flatteringly enough represented in the great classic texts of the West.

In dismissing this claim as made in bad faith, I could speak from my own experience as a Jew. The texts in question included very few *by* Jews, and whenever they referred *to* Jews or Judaism, it was more often than not in an unfriendly and even hostile spirit. Yet working through the two reading lists as a Columbia student, I felt that an

inheritance of indescribable richness which in the past had been in-
accessible to my own people (because of a combination of actual—
that is, legal—exclusion and voluntary isolation) was now mine for
the taking. Far from being left out, I was being invited *in,* and I
looked upon the invitation as a great opportunity and a privilege.

This did not preclude a sense of irony from time to time. Daniel
Bell himself once teased his future brother-in-law, the critic Alfred
Kazin, who at the age of twenty-five had written an amazingly precocious history of American literature entitled *On Native Grounds,*
for speaking of the American wilderness somewhere as "our
forests": "*Our* forests, Alfred?" (Kazin, who lacked the sense of humor that might have tempered the self-importance he shared with
Bell, was not amused.) In a similar vein, Sidney Morgenbesser, a
professor of philosophy at Columbia who was an ordained but
lapsed rabbi, once stopped dead in his tracks in the middle of a lecture about St. Augustine and asked his class whether they realized
how bizarre it was for a "nice Jewish boy" like him to be teaching
them about Christianity.

Like Bell and Morgenbesser, in the face of everything I believed
to the contrary, I could never quite get over the feeling that I was
not as "real" an American as someone whose people had come
here earlier than mine. Sometimes I would joke about this, as
when, in the early days of our marriage, my wife, who wrote (and
still does) under the name Midge Decter, and I drove one summer
to Fort Ticonderoga in upstate New York to visit what we thought
was an American shrine. But as we approached the gate, the first
thing we saw was a sign informing the public that this was the site
of several major battles in the French and Indian wars of the
1750s. "The French and Indian wars?" I burst out in mock indignation, "what's that got to do with me?" At this, in our ignorance,
we both giggled, and in an antic gesture of protest I turned the car
around without ever entering the fort. But when, many years later,
both of us read the great historian Francis Parkman's massive

work, *France and England in North America*, we found out that the answer to my stupid question was, "Everything."

On another occasion, I wrote that as the child of immigrants who came to this country as recently as the end of the nineteenth century, I personally felt as remote from the American Revolution as I did from the Wars of the Roses. I trusted that any intelligent reader would recognize this as an obviously extreme hyperbole, only to see it cited in an article of the 1980s by Gore Vidal in the far-Left weekly *The Nation* as proof that, in common with most Jews, my true loyalty was to Israel rather than to America.*

Passionate defender of Israel though I had indeed become when Vidal published that piece—and apart from everything else that was wrong with it—he could not have been more mistaken about my loyalty to America. In fact, those of my latter-day critics who accused me of being an American chauvinist were much closer to the mark. But loyalty aside, and even allowing for the occasional sense I had of the shallowness of my ancestral roots in this country, by the time I was graduated from Columbia and set sail for Cambridge, I had grown to feel (to lift a notorious simile from the Black Panther leader H. Rap Brown—for me, an unlikely source) "as American as cherry pie."

Spending three years in England, during which time I traveled widely in other countries as well, only intensified this feeling. In

---

*This article was entitled "The Empire Strikes Back." Here Vidal, in addition to resurrecting the old accusation of dual loyalty against the Jews (whom he portrayed as aliens living in America by the gracious sufferance of "the host country"), also conjured up the hoary idea of a malevolently conspiratorial Jewish power dangerous to everyone else. The only purpose of the Jews in America, he wrote, was "to make propaganda and raise money for Israel" (which he characterized as a "predatory people" and "an alien theocracy" engaged in "never-ending wars against just about everyone"). Stretching this absurd but poisonous charge even further, he de-

England itself, whose literature I knew and loved far better than I did the literature of America, and with whose past I was at least as familiar (never could I have made so silly an error as I subsequently would in my visit to Fort Ticonderoga about a site of comparable importance to English history), I was taken aback by how foreign a place it seemed; and I began thinking that maybe I was "one-hundred percent American" after all.

Much the same realization hit me in Israel when, in the summer of 1951, during the "long vac" from Cambridge, I first visited the infant Jewish state. This was even more surprising than my reaction to England, not merely because I was a Jew, but also because at that time I spoke and read Hebrew fluently, I loved the Bible (not as a believer but as a literary man), and I probably knew as much about the country, past and present, as I did about America.

That I should have been the possessor of such accomplishments was due to the gentle but firm pressure exerted on me by my father to continue my Jewish education way beyond the rudimentary instruction I began receiving at age six in the dingy little Hebrew school I attended for several hours every afternoon after "regular" school. Most Jewish kids of my generation in America went through the same training, but for them it ended at thirteen with a bar-mitzvah. This was not nearly enough to satisfy my father. Though he might have ceased observing most of the commandments that were binding upon Orthodox Jews and that he himself had been raised to live by, there was one commandment he did not

---

clared that the Jews were impoverishing the United States and bringing the world closer and closer to a nuclear war. Underlying the hatred and contempt of these words, moreover, was a strong tone of menace: now that he was revealing their secret, Vidal warned, the Jews (never mind if they had been born here or were naturalized citizens) had better watch out if they wished "to stay on among us." *Us!* Given all this—and more—no wonder "The Empire Strikes Back" impressed me and many other readers as the most blatantly and egregiously anti-Semitic outburst to have appeared in a respectable American periodical since World War Two.

fail to keep: "Thou shalt teach them to thy sons." The "them" in this biblical verse, repeatedly recited in the daily prayers, refers to the laws of Moses, but for him (and he was very far from alone in this) it meant the language and literature of the Jewish people he loved, as the same passage commands one to love God, with all his heart and all his soul and all his might.

The result was that, under protest, I agreed to attend a Hebrew high school two nights a week (again after "regular" school) and every Sunday as well. Then, upon graduation from that institution, and once more under protest, I enrolled in the Jewish Theological Seminary—not to study for the rabbinate but to enter the academic division, then called the College of Jewish Studies, contained within the institution. There too I spent two long nights a week and all day Sunday, ultimately earning the degree of Bachelor of Hebrew Literature even as I was being awarded a B.A. at Columbia, which I had been working for all along at the same time during the day.

As only a year had passed since my graduation from the College of Jewish Studies when I first visited Israel, I had every reason to think that I would feel at home in what was (as the Balfour Declaration of 1919 had promised) now a homeland for the Jewish people who had been in exile for two thousand years. Yet six weeks there finished what a year in England had inaugurated. No doubt the Jewish people had been in exile, but not *this* Jew, not me. *My* true homeland was America, and the Jewish homeland was, so far as I was concerned, a foreign country. Like England, it was a country to which I was closely related, and I was very happy that it had been established as a sovereign state to which persecuted Jews in need of refuge could flee, as millions of them, and at the cost of their lives, had been unable to do only a short while back. But I could not imagine any such thing ever happening to me, or to the Jews of America in general; and if, God forbid, it ever did and I was forced to settle in Israel, I would almost certainly feel that I was *now* in exile.

When with my big mouth I told this to the Israelis I met—passionate Zionists all—they were always shocked and even offended.* They had every right to be, so tactless was it of me to utter such sentiments to people who were still living in harsh physical conditions and struggling with all their energies to make something of the state they had only three years earlier gone to war (against the combined might of five Arab armies) to prevent from being slaughtered in its cradle. But to be fair to myself, I only opened that big mouth in the first place because they kept attacking me as immoral and as a bad Jew for refusing to move to Israel.

Anyhow, these Israeli Zionists were dead wrong in their opinion of why I (a stand-in for the entire American Jewish community) had no wish to settle in Israel. Socialists almost to a man, they were convinced that we were simply too "materialistic," too deeply sunk in the flesh pots of a rich country, to make the sacrifices in our standard of living that emigrating to Israel would entail. Many of them, not without a certain vindictiveness or *Schadenfreude*, were also convinced that we would eventually be forced to do so anyway: why should America turn out to be different from Germany, whose Jews once believed, just as we Americans now did, that they had found a true home there?†

---

*Not even in their worst nightmares could these people have dreamed that many of their own children and grandchildren would turn into "post-Zionists" who would question the very legitimacy of Israel as a Jewish state and would speak and write of it with a hostility no less fierce than that of their country's Arab enemies.

†Indeed, this is exactly how many Jewish refugees from Germany who were then living in Israel still felt about their country of origin (though nothing analogous could be detected among those who had come from East Europe or the Muslim world). Not even Hitler and the Nazis could prevent these *yekkes*, as they were derisively called in Hebrew slang, from pining for their old German homes, from believing that German culture was superior to all others, and from pitying themselves for having landed in so dismal a backwater as Israel.

No, the real reason America was my home had little or nothing to do with the higher material standard of living it afforded (or rather might some day afford) me. But it did have much—maybe even everything—to do with my passion for the English language. Countless others might have successfully moved from one language into another, some of them (like the Pole Joseph Conrad and, later, the Russian Vladimir Nabokov) even becoming great virtuosos in the use of English. Yet reasonably fluent though I then was in Hebrew, I doubted that I would ever be able to master it, get to the bottom of it, penetrate its inner spirit, as I felt confident I was doing with English. Already I had succeeded in having two pieces of literary criticism professionally published, and I was also naturally articulate in speech. The exercise of those powers gave me so much delight that to lose them would be like losing my arms or my legs; and to do this voluntarily, which is what my Israeli interlocutors were demanding, would be like cutting them off myself.

Why then did I also rule out living in England, as I had an opportunity to when I was offered a teaching fellowship at Clare, my Cambridge college, in an almost certain prelude to a permanent position? The answer I would have given had I been asked that question would have approximated George Bernard Shaw's crack that the English and the Americans were two peoples separated by a common language. Having grown up in America, I felt at home there to a degree that I gradually came to realize I never could or would in England, whose strangeness increased rather than decreased for me with each passing year.

And yet, that common language to which Shaw had referred, and which, to say it yet again, had greater importance for me than almost anything else, was an inheritance more from England than from America itself. Not just ultimately—in the sense that the English language had been brought to America from England—but even immediately. For where literature was concerned, it was England's, and not America's, in which I felt most at home. I knew more of it, I knew it better, and I prized it more. There was nothing in American literature—or any other, for that matter—to compare with Shakespeare. Nor were there any American poets as great as (to name only a few) John Donne, John Milton, Alexander Pope, and John Keats in past centuries, and W. B. Yeats (Irish though he might have been) in our own. As for Yeats's closest rival, T. S. Eliot, though born in St. Louis, he was more English than American, and so was the great American contender in the field of fiction, Henry James. Except for the best of James's novels, there were only a few others written in America (especially Nathaniel Hawthorne's *The Scarlet Letter*, Herman Melville's *Moby-Dick*, Mark Twain's *Adventures of Huckleberry Finn*, and Theodore Dreiser's *An American Tragedy*) that for my money ranked with the supreme masterpieces produced by Jane Austen, Charles Dickens, George Eliot, Anthony Trollope, and a dozen more.

In later years, when the Library of America's beautiful and scrupulously scholarly editions of the American classics began being published, I was enticed into revisiting some I had not looked at in ages and into reading others for the first time that I had missed in my youth. I had missed them, as I have already noted, partly because when I was an undergraduate at Columbia, there were only a few cursory courses in American literature, and it was even possible to graduate with a major in English without taking any of them. (I took only one, and a short one at that.) The general attitude was much the same as I have just given as my own: that, with a few notable exceptions, the American novelists and poets were vastly inferior to those of England (and also France and Russia, though not necessarily any of the other European countries). Hence, anyone interested in literature as such was better off devoting himself to the major Europeans, while consulting the Americans mainly for what they had to teach about the nature of the native soul.

I still think there was some truth in this judgment, but it undoubtedly reflected too great a readiness to acquiesce in the assumption of European superiority, and there was a good deal of unseemly and unhealthy self-denigration in it as well. "It's a complex fate, being an American," said Henry James himself, who knew what he was talking about on this subject if anyone did. Everyone, including me, always used to quote this remark, but hardly anyone paid attention to what followed it in the very same sentence: "and one of the responsibilities it entails is fighting against a superstitious valuation of Europe." Even leaving aside invidious comparisons with European culture, however, it was not for its celebration of America and American life, but precisely for its sourness toward the society from which it emerged, that American literature was most often esteemed by critics like Alfred Kazin and Richard Chase, who had only recently begun making the case for its intrinsic literary interest and importance.

These critics argued that American literature provided, as it were, concrete documentation to vindicate the hostility toward America on both Left and Right that arose in the immediate aftermath of the Civil War (in the so-called "Gilded Age") and that spread inexorably through the literary culture over the next hundred years. And the critics were right: most American novelists *did* agree with or take their cue from "muckraking" journalists of the post–Civil War era like Ida Tarbell on the one side and conservative intellectuals like Henry Adams on the other in portraying their own society as corrupt, vulgar, philistine, materialistic, and puritanical.*

By the time I began revisiting this literature, I had "broken ranks" with the Left, and had then spent two decades and more arguing against the same charges by the contemporary avatars of the writers who had originally made them. I was therefore at first a lit-

---

*The concept of an "adversary culture," on which Chase and Kazin leaned, was developed most forcefully by the somewhat older critic Lionel Trilling, who, however, was more ambivalent about it than they were. I go more thoroughly into the issues involved in the sections below.

tle abashed to discover when I read or reread these older writers in their elegant Library of America incarnations that the indictment, so hollow in its updated versions, still rang true in the original.

But there really was nothing to be abashed about here. It was clear that the older writers were accurately, if more than a bit one-sidedly, describing the country they lived in. Yet it was no less clear that their epigones seemed not to have noticed that the country *they* lived in was a very different place, or that many of the abuses of which their literary forefathers complained had been corrected through political action in the ensuing decades. Moreover, unlike the current crop, most of the older writers, even after becoming disillusioned or disenchanted, retained a degree of respect, fondness, and even love for the world out of which they came. I am thinking in particular of Willa Cather and Sarah Orne Jewett, but also of Frank Norris, Jack London, and even, most unexpectedly, Sinclair Lewis (especially in *Main Street*, whose affection for America is one of the qualities that makes it superior to the more famous but less complex *Babbitt*).

Another point: as a consequence in part of the limitations put by political action on their power, but also in (larger?) part of the ridicule heaped upon them by Lewis and the others, the real-life models of the businessmen and the boosters and the "solid citizens" of Main Street and Babbitt's Zenith gradually lost their confidence. In time they even humbly gave way to the very people George F. Babbitt himself had denounced as "these blabber-mouth, fault-finding, pessimistic, cynical University teachers" and "the long-haired gentry who call themselves 'liberals' and 'radicals' . . ."

Yet when America came to live with the results of this profound shift in cultural power, some of us began wondering whether it was so clear that Babbitt was wrong and his creator right. Was it really so self-evident that the country was better off under the influence of its "enlightened" cultural elites than it was when—again in Babbitt's words—

The ideal of American manhood and culture [wasn't] a lot of cranks sitting around chewing the rag about their Rights and Wrongs, but a God-fearing, hustling, successful two-fisted Regular Guy . . . who plays hard and works hard, and whose answer to his critics is a square-toed boot that'll teach the grouches and smart alecks to respect the He-man and get out and root for Uncle Samuel, U.S.A.!

It was easy enough in the early decades of the twentieth century to echo Sinclair Lewis and his even more vituperative champion H. L. Mencken in ridiculing this kind of talk. It was not so easy as the century came to a close.

T he main thing I wish to stress here, however, is the gratification it afforded me, as a great lover of America, to discover on making my way through its literary classics when I was already in my sixties that from a strictly literary point of view, more richness was lurking there than I had realized or imagined when I was in my twenties and thirties. American literature was still not to be placed on a par with the literature of England, but neither was it to be dismissed as wholly second-rate or merely derivative; and at its very best, it could hold its head up high in the company of the great British writers.

Later, I will try to explain why this fact has more than a strictly aesthetic significance—why, that is, it represents a kind of bonus that very few observers of the "American experiment" ever expected this country to collect on top of the "life, liberty, and pursuit of happiness" it was explicitly designed to ensure. But for the moment, I want to return to where I began—that remedial-speech class to which I was assigned as a small child in a Brooklyn public school. In making me conscious of the sound and the music of the English language, the training I received there powerfully reinforced my ability to claim the literary and cultural inheritance that was mine simply by virtue of having been born in America.

Because of bilingualism—the demented and discredited theory that the best way to teach English to children from homes in which Spanish or Chinese or some other language is spoken is to conduct their classes in those other languages—many millions who came or were born here in the last decades of the twentieth century were subjected to the opposite experience from mine. Instead of being helped to share in their inheritance as Americans, they were beset by obstacles blocking their path to it. As I was blessed, so were they cursed, and as I was enriched, so were they impoverished.

I should note that just as the twentieth century was drawing to a close, a study issued by the National Immigration Forum reported that three out of four of the newer immigrants were speaking English "well" within ten years of arriving in the United States. I felt slightly reassured upon reading this, but I could not help suspecting that what the report meant by "well" fell far short of the degree of proficiency these immigrants would have needed to absorb the literary heritage that was made as accessible as possible to my own generation. Nor did I place much credence in similar reports purporting to prove that bilingualism was working and that the children subjected to it were learning English more quickly than they would otherwise have done. Even if these mostly self-interested assessments had not been contradicted by the evidence even of official statistics, they simply ran afoul of common sense.

On the other hand, what was genuinely reassuring was the victory in California of the campaign led by Ron Unz for Proposition 227 mandating the replacement of bilingual education with a year of English immersion. Making a mockery of dire predictions about the harm this would do to the children, improvement was even more dramatic than supporters of Proposition 227 had hoped. The children absorbed English so rapidly, and test scores in various subjects went up so steeply, that even some former opponents were forced to concede that they had been wrong in hold-ing out for bilingualism. Meanwhile, wrote the syndicated colum-nist Matthew Miller, "fewer than ten percent of those [parents] with limited-English students in L.A. schools . . . sought waivers to return their kids to bilingual classes," as the new system allowed them to do.* In spite of all this, the bilingual interests would not give up their fight to repeal Proposition 227 by challenging it in the courts.

If Hebrew, as all the monotheistic religions deriving from the Bible would agree, is God's first language, then English, I have often thought (secretly until now), must be His second. Otherwise how would such miracles as Shakespeare and the King James Bible have become possible? The Yale polymath David Gelernter, in a piece in *National Review*, speaks precisely to this question in dis-cussing contemporary translations into English (including one he has been working on himself) of the David stories in the two books of Samuel in the Hebrew Bible. These stories, he correctly states, "are one of mankind's finest literary achievements," and the He-brew prose in which they are told has "incomparable artistic power." But, he goes on,

> The translator into English has at his disposal the richest, most sensitive instrument ever invented for tuning in and cap-turing literary thought. Other Western languages are cheap transistor radios as compared with the monumentally sensi-tive radio telescope of English, which can pick up faint nu-ances originating thousands of years ago.

---

*There was nothing surprising about this, since (as Unz, basing himself on offi-cial state statistics, wrote in *Commentary* of the bilugual regime) "a full quarter of all children in California public schools were classified as not knowing English, and 95 percent of these children failed to learn English in any given year."

But whether or not Gelernter is being a little unfair to other Western languages, and whether or not I am right that English is God's second language,* it has definitely become the second language of the entire human world. Writing in the *City Journal*, Theodore Dalrymple says it all:

> English is . . . an instrument of marvelous subtlety and absorptive capacity, capable simultaneously of the greatest flights of poetry and the clearest expression of science and metaphysics. English literature is undoubtedly one of the greatest in human history, and it gave to the world its only truly universal poet and playwright.

Which is why I continually thank my lucky stars for having been born into and then having been taught to avail myself of the miraculous glories embodied in this marvelous instrument. And the more I do so, the more my heart goes out to the children of immigrants who came here nearly a century after my own parents did, and the angrier I grow at the adults who (in no small measure motivated by the latest mutation of the anti-Americanism that refuses to die) were robbing or cheating them of the blessings of this inheritance, and fighting like tigers against any policy that would encourage them to reach out with both arms and gather in as much of what is rightfully theirs as they had the will and the capability to do.

---

*Amusingly, George Bernard Shaw in his play *Pygmalion* has Henry Higgins declaring (and the same words are repeated in the Lerner-Loewe musical adaptation, *My Fair Lady*) that "English is the language of Shakespeare and the Bible." In a more serious vein, the biblical scholar and translator Robert Alter of Berkeley observes of the King James Version that it renders "Hebrew idioms in English as though they had always been indigenous English idioms."

PART

II

The Making of a Patriot

Bishop Talleyrand is reputed to have said that anyone who had not lived in France before the revolution of 1789 could not know the meaning of "*le plaisir de vivre*," the pleasure of living.* Of course, born as he was into the high nobility, Talleyrand had every reason to look back nostalgically on the *ancien régime*, with the delights and privileges it afforded members of his class. Besides, he had added to those delights and privileges great personal distinction of his own in becoming perhaps the leading statesman in France of the time.

I have brought Talleyrand in here because I myself would make a claim for the world of my childhood and early youth that is in one respect similar to his. To be sure, I am fully conscious of the incongruity, and of how strange it must seem to perceive any resemblance whatsoever between "the pleasure of living" for an aristocrat in pre-revolutionary France and my own "underprivileged" existence in a period that is generally regarded, and with very good reason, as one of the worst of times in a century that offered a plethora of terrible rivals to choose from.

I was born, after all, into circumstances almost as far distant on the social and economic spectrum as it is possible to get from Talleyrand's: a working-class family at the beginning of the Great De-

---

*Not (according to the *Oxford Dictionary of Quotations*) "*la douceur de la vie*," the sweetness of life, as the saying has often been incorrectly quoted, including by me.

pression. Though the fact that my father had a job saved us from the shame of "going on relief," we were still very poor in all but the essentials. Millions upon millions of other Americans lacked even so much as those, since with a few ups and downs the Depression lasted (notwithstanding hagiographical claims made of a cure by President Franklin D. Roosevelt's New Deal) until another great war broke out in 1939. It was only then that American factories started coming back to life, as orders poured in from Europe for arms and ammunition.

This is not to deny that the New Deal can be credited with establishing a "safety net," which—before Lyndon Johnson was to turn it thirty years later into a welfare system that would do more harm than good by keeping its intended beneficiaries in a condition of dependency from one generation to the next—alleviated some of the worst effects of the Depression. Roosevelt also devoted himself to strengthening the labor movement—a policy that was derided by his opponents as "Clear it with Sidney" (meaning that he supposedly never made a move without getting the labor leader Sidney Hillman to sign off on it first). Yet whether inadvertently or by a deliberate design of killing with kindness, Roosevelt's pro-labor policies arguably helped to undermine the development in the United States of the kind of socialist movement that swelled the power of the unions in England to the point where they would have to be cut down to size by Prime Minister Margaret Thatcher in the 1980s before the British economy could be modernized and vitalized.

Still, neither the safety net nor the legislation strengthening the labor movement ever did more than palliate the economic miseries in which the country was mired when Roosevelt was sworn in as President in January 1933. By 1937, things had improved somewhat, but there was a relapse in the following year, from which it took the orders from abroad in 1939 to begin rescuing the economy. What finally did the trick were the prodigious feats of production made necessary by the entry of the United States itself into the war in 1941. This, combined with the absorption of what eventually amounted to a total of about sixteen million men into all branches of the armed forces, put a complete end to the epidemic of joblessness that had afflicted the United States for ten long years. But the subsequent death and maiming of so many of those men was a high price to pay for economic recovery. Even a "good war" like the one against Hitler and his allies was no bed of roses, as a movie of the late 1990s like Steven Spielberg's *Saving Private Ryan*—with its unflinching depiction of the spilled guts and severed limbs that it cost to launch the invasion of the European continent on D-Day of 1944—demonstrated to anyone who still harbored any romantic illusions on that score.

I am not, God forbid, suggesting that the United States went to war in 1941 as a way of stimulating a depressed economy. This was the very suggestion made afterward by Marxists intent on proving that the capitalist system, in accordance with their master's theory, had been exposed as unviable by the Depression, and who were desperately trying to show that it would have suffered a knockout blow if it had not been saved by the bell of the war. All the more desperate did these Marxists become when the depression they had predicted would roar back in full force with the demobilization of the country—the shutting down of the armaments factories, and then all those millions of soldiers returning to civilian life and looking for jobs—never materialized. Instead, a new degree of prosperity seemed to be in the process of creating what the economist John Kenneth Galbraith would by 1958 label "the affluent society" (and, where affluence was concerned, neither he nor anyone else had seen anything yet).

At a loss for an explanation, the Marxists floundered for about two years, trying out this theory and playing around with that, until—Eureka!—the cold war began, and they were happily back in business at the same old stand. In their interpretation of its outbreak in 1947, the United States under Roosevelt's successor, Harry Truman, had an ulterior motive and a secret agenda. The peace-loving Soviet Union was portrayed by Washington as an expansionist threat not because it actually believed so preposterous an idea about its erstwhile ally in the war against Hitler. No: the real reason was, said the Marxists, to put the American economy back on a wartime basis so as to forestall the new depression lurking in the wings and the final demise of capitalism that would come with it.

But there I go again, getting ahead of my story, which at this juncture is about the years immediately preceding the war and those of the war itself. No doubt it was difficult for later generations to imagine the pleasure of life experienced by the aristocracy in pre-revolutionary France. Yet it is probably harder, and perhaps even impossible, for anyone who never lived through the 1930s in America to imagine the extent and the intensity of the love Americans of every stripe felt for their country in spite of the hardships of the Great Depression and those of the war that followed hard upon it.

Obviously, a distinction has to be made between the two sets of hardship and the responses to them. That World War Two did not prevent, and even further stimulated, the arousal of patriotic passions neither was nor is a mystery—except to a large and influential segment of the Vietnam generation, whose hysterically negative response to *its* war was untypical. But even some of these people finally unraveled the mystery. By the end of the twentieth century, it was being proclaimed all over the place that the men who had fought in World War Two were—as the anchor of the NBC Nightly News program, Tom Brokaw, unqualifiedly honored them in a best-selling book—the "greatest generation" ever to have been produced by America.

This was the very championship title that had previously been bestowed on the *anti*-war young of the Vietnam period who, to the near-universal applause of their parents, teachers, and media sycophants, had been celebrated by an eminent Harvard professor as "the best informed, the most intelligent, and the most idealistic this country has ever known." In taking the accolade away from them and awarding it instead to the soldiers of World War Two, Brokaw's book was signaling, one might say, "a return to normalcy" (as measured by how almost all countries in most ages and places have felt about the men who risk or lose their lives fighting for the homeland) in the climate of American opinion.

But what on the other hand was and remains a mystery is why people should have revered the country even during the Great Depression, when it was putting them through so much deprivation and pain that, unlike the sacrifices they would make during the war, were untempered by the glories and heroics of a struggle that the vast majority of Americans regarded as one of good against evil.

I have no easy answer, but the fact is that this is how it was, at least after 1935. Certain liberal hagiographers would have us believe that Roosevelt, nominated by the Democrats in 1932 to the tune of "Happy Days Are Here Again," had then lifted the nation's fallen spirits from the moment he was inaugurated as President with his unforgettable—and unforgotten—assurance that "The only thing we have to fear is fear itself." Then, these same hagiographers tell us, he had cheered everyone up even more by setting his New Deal into motion, thereby instilling hope for the future in a people on the brink of losing it forever.

That there is some truth in this version of events I would not dream of denying. Even as that little boy of five or six sitting in a remedial-speech class, I became aware of a special excitement in the air connected with "President Roosevelt" (the only President I would know until I reached the age of fifteen and whose name in my own household was always spoken in a tone of hushed reverence and never without the title attached).

The excitement I am talking about was generated by the Blue Eagle, the symbol of the NRA (the National Recovery Administration), one of the first agencies created by the new President.

The NRA's purpose was to forge an alliance among the government, the corporations, and the unions that would get the silenced factories humming again, but it turned out to be ineffective. What was even more embarrassing, the concept behind it bore an uncomfortable resemblance to the theory of the "corporate state" that underpinned the thinking of the fascists who were ruling Italy under Benito Mussolini. After about two years, the "fair-practice" codes established by the NRA were (rightly, and apparently to Roosevelt's own relief) declared unconstitutional by the Supreme Court, and soon relegated to the ash heap of misbegotten experiments.*

While it lasted, the fanfare accompanying the NRA was pleasantly deafening. Possibly the impression left over from my early childhood is—like my mother's memory of her "rich" uncle in Galicia—exaggerated and too highly colored. Yet (it is my earliest political recollection) I am reasonably certain that the Blue Eagle was everywhere; and I mean everywhere. It was hung on posters in school, it was printed on special stamps, banners bearing it were waved in parades, and armbands displaying it were handed out and proudly worn. Too young to have any idea of what it symbolized, I still somehow developed a great affection for that eagle, which in some odd way (and as a tribute to the power of even fairly primitive political propaganda) is with me even now.

But if neither the NRA nor any of the experiments that accompanied or followed it brought about more than a mild economic improvement, Roosevelt himself was never blamed. As one historian has correctly observed, "Millions of suffering Americans, spawn of an individualist culture, blamed themselves for their plight." But as we have already seen, so did others who had come

---

*Some of the New Deal's later pro-labor laws, however, were based on certain provisions of the NRA, and survived after being reenacted on their own.

to America from cultures that were not individualist at all. Somehow, they felt, it was their fault that they were unable to find jobs; and as for Roosevelt, at least he was *trying*, and this alone seemed to lift the national mood. True, there were those on the Right who hated this scion of the American aristocracy with all their hearts as "a traitor to his class," and even suspected him of secretly trying to establish a dictatorial socialist, or even Communist, regime in the country. But they were hopelessly outnumbered by his devotees, to some of whom he was like a god. Hence when he ran for reelection in 1936, even with unemployment still very high, he won by a huge landslide against the hapless governor of Kansas, Alf Landon, who had been sent by the Republicans on a political suicide mission to run against him.

An amusing light on the importance that was attached to Roosevelt's reelection (and here I come to my second earliest political memory) is that someone circulated the rumor throughout P.S. 28 that if Landon became President, he would make us go to school on Saturdays. Where this rumor came from I am at a complete loss to tell. Probably it was a fantasy the kids themselves concocted as the only thing they could think of that would give them a personal stake in the election. But who knows? Conceivably some political operative was behind it, imagining that it would get the children to frighten their ignorant immigrant parents (particularly the Sabbath-observing Orthodox Jews among them) into voting for Roosevelt. If so, it was a total waste of time, since each and every one of our parents was for him anyway, and nothing could have persuaded them to support anyone against FDR, let alone the colorless Alf Landon.*

Other important factors were at work in the heightening of na-

---

*This may not have been entirely true of the Italians. Though, like the Irish, they were all Catholics, ethnicity trumped religion in the relations between the two groups. At that time, the Irish still dominated the Democratic political machines in New York and other big cities. Because they had come to this country

tional morale that Roosevelt brought about in spite of the persistence of mass unemployment. To begin with, there was his cheerful and optimistic personality.* Television had not yet been invented, but the President could frequently be seen in newspaper photographs and newsreels in the movie theaters, and usually he would be wearing a big grin on his face with a cigarette holder clenched at a cocky angle between his teeth.

Then there were his legendary "fireside chats" on the radio. He would use these to explain himself and his policies, but also to radiate the high spirits that were so essential a part of his nature that they could not even be dampened by the paralyzed condition in which his legs had been left by an attack of polio years earlier. He made a great point of showing that he could stand on his own two feet behind a rostrum, and also tried to keep his disability hidden under a blanket and out of sight whenever he appeared in, say, a

---

knowing English, the Irish had enjoyed a head start in politics over the other immigrant groups who followed, and they naturally reserved most of the patronage they controlled for their own. The special resentments this bred among the Italians led a relatively large number of them (at least in New York) into becoming Republicans, the only major Catholic or ethnic group who did. It was out of this tradition that politicians like Alfonse D'Amato would come. Eventually, however, the Italians finally got a strong enough foothold in the New York Democratic machine to elect one of their own, Carmine DeSapio, as leader of Tammany Hall. Taking advantage of their recently acquired power, the new Democratic political bosses put so many Italians on the benches of the city and state courts that Daniel Patrick Moynihan, writing as a political scientist before entering electoral politics himself, could quip that by the early 1960s, "the ennui was showing even among the Italians" themselves.

*Ronald Reagan, who began his political life as a Democrat and never stopped admiring Roosevelt even after going over to the Republicans, had a similar quality. What is more, he used it to much the same effect in reviving the sagging post-Vietnam American will to resume the fight against Soviet Communism as Roosevelt had in raising the national spirits during the Depression. There is good reason to think that in this, Reagan was not only doing what came naturally but following the model created by his old hero.

motorcade. But everyone knew that he wore steel leg braces and even then could only support himself by leaning heavily on canes. My guess is that an encouraging psychological effect flowed from the sheer existence of a man who, like the country he led, was crippled (to use the now politically incorrect word that was then current) and yet refused to let it get him down. He truly was what he himself had called his sometime rival (and future enemy), Governor Al Smith of New York, in nominating him for President at the Democratic convention of 1928—a "happy warrior."

Finally, there was a factor beyond Roosevelt's own control that contributed both to the surprisingly good cheer of the period and also to the fervent patriotism that flourished at a time when very bitter resentment against the country might have been expected to develop instead. This special factor took shape not in Washington but in Moscow, and it had a profound effect on the atmosphere over here.

To understand why, it is necessary first to recognize that throughout Roosevelt's first term, the Right was not the only political force in America that feared and loathed him. He was no less an object of hatred on the far Left, then dominated by the Communist party, whose ranks had understandably been swelled by the Depression. If the Right was mistaken in believing that Roosevelt was out to destroy capitalism, the Communists were correctly convinced that his objective was to save it. Hence, during the so-called "Third Period" of their own history, which overlapped with Roosevelt's first term in office, the American Communist party (CPUSA), acting, as we now know for certain, under instructions from the Soviet dictator Joseph Stalin, treated him as a dangerous enemy. The order of the day for the CP was to preach and do whatever it could to organize a revolution against the moribund bourgeois order in America which the new President was working to prop up.

Why, the man from Mars, or from "a generation that knew not [this particular] Joseph," might ask, was it necessary to make a revolution in order to bring down a system that was supposedly dying anyway? Because even though in Marxist theory the doom of capitalism was historically inevitable, and even though the Depression showed that the day of judgment was at hand for this unjust and unworkable system, giving an extra push could do no harm. It might even prevent the delay in the inevitable collapse which Roosevelt, in his ignorant and maddeningly insouciant fashion, was trying to create.

This extra push took the form of unremitting attacks on American capitalism and its allegedly phony façade of democracy: in reality, the line went, America was a political brother under the skin to the openly fascist regimes in Germany and Italy. Such attacks were by no means effective enough to diminish Roosevelt's political popularity among voters at large. Yet, through their influence over many writers and intellectuals, the Communists did inject a strong current of doubt about America itself into the cultural atmosphere. As it had been before and would be again later, most writers and intellectuals in the 1930s were on the Left, and even many who were liberals or socialists rather than members of the CP fell under its ideological sway early in that decade in spite of the fact that, to the Communists of the day, these people were actually "social fascists" and "running dogs of capitalism."*

Swallowing such insults, a long list of distinguished literary people and other intellectuals, including non-Communists like the

---

*From the Communist point of view, the socialists, as ideological schismatics, were worse than the liberals (just as, in the eyes of orthodox religious believers, heretics are always worse than members of other religions because they sow confusion about the faith). This attitude found classical comic expression in a satirical song written by some anonymous genius. It was about how one labor union in the garment trade that was controlled by Communists saw an anti-Stalinist rival in the same industry: "Oh, the cloak makers' union is a no good union, / Is a right-wing

literary critic Edmund Wilson, had signed a statement in 1932 urging support of the Communist candidate who was running against Roosevelt and the incumbent President, Herbert Hoover. Then, during Roosevelt's first term, came a spate of novels like John Steinbeck's *In Dubious Battle*, plays like Clifford Odets's *Waiting for Lefty*, and a plethora of movies in which America was represented by the vicious capitalist who was pitted against the virtuous, even saintly, Communist (often a union organizer).

Literally overnight, however, all this changed. By 1935, Stalin was becoming apprehensive about the growing power of the new Nazi regime that Hitler had established upon becoming chancellor of Germany in 1933. Thinking it the better part of prudence to forge a *de facto* alliance with the Western democracies to discourage Hitler from going after the Soviet Union, Stalin sent the word forth from the Kremlin to his followers in America (and everywhere else as well) to call off the dogs of revolution. Fascist at heart no more, the bourgeois democracies were from now on—or at any rate for the time being—to be treated as allies of the Communists *against* fascism.

In implementing this new "Popular Front" strategy, Communists were instructed to stop acting like revolutionaries. Instead they were to portray themselves as no different from the formerly despised liberals except in their impatience to bring about the same reforms: they were "liberals in a hurry." And far from representing a threat to the country, or from being the instrument of a foreign power, Communism itself was—in the words of Earl Browder, then

---

union for the boss / (Gyp! Gyp!). / Oh, the socialist fakers in the dirty cloak makers / Give the workers a dirty double-cross / (Gyp! Gyp!). / Then come the Hillquits and the Thomases, / They fool the workers with false promises. / Oh, they preach socialism / But they practice fascism / To save capitalism / For the boss (Gyp! Gyp!)." Morris Hillquit was one of the founders of the Socialist party in America and a perennial candidate for Congress from New York. Norman Thomas later became the national leader of the party, and its perennial candidate for President.

the leader of the CPUSA—a wholly indigenous product of America: "twentieth-century Americanism," to use the slogan he and his comrades and their fellow-travelers now adopted.

My grandmother Esther Malkah would later curse Uncle Sam for drafting her son into the army, but the Communists now went to almost comical lengths in dressing themselves up to look like him. Everything they did was made to seem as American as possible. What had been the Young Communist League one day became on the very next American Youth for Democracy (AYD), whose local chapters now named themselves after legendary figures from American history like Molly Pitcher or Paul Revere. The "educational" institution the party set up in New York was called the Jefferson School of Social Science. When men were recruited by the CP to fight against Hitler's ally Franco in the Spanish Civil War, it was the Lincoln Brigade they were asked to join. When party literary hacks like Howard Fast wrote novels, they were now likely to be about heroes of the American Revolution, albeit the more radical ones (my own favorite in this genre was *Citizen Tom Paine*).

It was out of the imperatives of this ethos too that American folk music was popularized through the agency of party members or sympathizers like Woody Guthrie and Pete Seeger. Last but by no means least, on the radio and in Hollywood, Communists in liberal clothing, with the help of non-Communists like the director Frank Capra (who was either taken in by the party's deceptions or driven by his own naïve political predilections) did their best to blur the distinction between liberalism and Communism by drawing on the powerful populist strain in American history. This was what happened in hugely successful Capra films like *Mr. Smith Goes to Washington* (whose screenplay, in a typical example of the Popular Front process at work, was written by a not-so-secret member of the Communist party) and *Meet John Doe* (which did not come out until 1941, but was set in the late 1930s and was also a pure product of the Popular Front mentality of that period).

In both of these movies, the emphasis was on the enemy all good Americans were up against: the wicked capitalists (always, it seemed, played by the corpulent Edward Arnold) whose private armies were prepared to take over our beloved country, abolish our freedoms, and set themselves up as our rulers. These villains were on the point of succeeding when the ordinary Joe (James Stewart or Gary Cooper) would step in and manage to save the day to the strains of a speech about the glories of American democracy and the wonderful decency of the people it bred.

The net result of the Popular Front strategy was to silence the vituperative assaults on this country that would otherwise have continued coming from the Left. God knows that there was more than enough in the economic realities of the period to make for an ugly public mood without any help from the Communists or anyone else. Nonetheless, if the steady drumbeat of such assaults had gone on, it surely would to some indeterminate extent have reinforced and deepened this mood. But as it was, the Communists now ironically did their bit to reverse the "revolutionary situation" that they themselves were only yesterday certain the Depression had created and whose development they had been doing their best to urge forward at a faster clip.

And so it was that patriotism was mother's milk to a kid like me precisely when I might so easily have been brought up on some curdled and sour brew. I may not have had a clue as to what I was saying when I sang "Holy, Holy, Holy" in school, but I certainly knew what I was affirming when I took the pledge of allegiance to the flag of America every morning and to the republic for which it stood. And even if, when I joined in the choruses of "Columbia, the Gem of the Ocean" or "America the Beautiful," not to mention "The Star-Spangled Banner," I would not yet have been able to define some of the words any better than I could those of "Holy, Holy, Holy" (what could "amber waves of grain" or "purple mountain majesties" have meant to me, who had never been farther from Brooklyn than the Bronx or Jersey City?), I understood full well and swelled to the sentiments I was lustily expressing. America, "from sea to shining sea," was the greatest country in the world, "the land of the brave and the free," and I was lucky to have been born here.

Then in 1939 the Soviet Union made its notorious pact with Nazi Germany. At the age of nine, I was much too young to experience the enormous trauma this incredible and infamous agreement inflicted on so many people, whether Communist-party members or fellow-travelers or only mild sympathizers. Indeed, I cannot say with any confidence that I was even conscious of what had happened, except that a dim sense comes back to me now of my father's fury over it as a Jew and a Zionist. The very opposite of a joiner, and temperamentally averse to activism of any kind, he was never a Zionist in the way my future wife's parents were in St. Paul, Minnesota. Midge's mother, Rose Calmenson (born in St. Paul), was a leader of Hadassah, the women's Zionist organization, and Midge's father, Harry Rosenthal (an immigrant like mine, but one who had broken out of the family cocoon in New York to seek his fortune in an even stranger and more foreign place), was an early member of the Zionist Organization of America. He never became a really rich man, but, after a number of false starts in business, he eventually got a successful sporting-goods store going which would then thrive after the war on army-surplus items that were useful to local hunters and fishermen.

In leaving New York, incidentally, my future father-in-law was bravely following a trail that had been blazed by much braver Jewish immigrants before him. These were people who were more venturesome and—in some crude Darwinian sense—more fitted for survival in America than my own pitifully timid and less energetic family, who stayed put where they landed and continued huddling together and clinging to one another for dear life. They were punished for this by becoming among the few Jews who remained poor in America. In another of the many deviations from the socioeconomic stereotypes of the American Jewish community that marked my own background, just one member of my family, my father's older brother, uncle Nathan, ever made any money to speak of, and he was the only one who left New York. In flight from a cousin he was expected to marry after a stint in the American army in World War One, he took himself all the way to San Francisco, where he became a successful herbal pharmacist (though not nearly so successful as he would have been at a later date when his kind of "natural" remedies would become all the rage).

But in thus climbing steadily up the greasy economic pole, neither my uncle Nathan nor my future father-in-law was a match for the Jewish peddlers who, beginning in colonial times and continuing through the nineteenth century, had set out in covered wagons to sell furs, dry goods, and household items to pioneers living wherever the frontier happened to be at any given moment, and to the Indians as well.

To take the full measure of the courage and grit of these people, one has to bear in mind that many of them were, when they started out, religiously observant (or what we would today call Orthodox). This meant not only that they had to carry their phylacteries and prayer shawls and prayer books with them for daily use, but that they had to find ways of adhering to the dietary laws under conditions which made this enormously difficult, kosher butchers not exactly being a standard feature of the American frontier.

After a while, most gave up, but not all. Louis Berg, in two fascinating accounts published in *Commentary*, gave some examples of the more obdurate. One was a fur trader in colonial Philadelphia:

Bernard Gratz, whose portrait, painted by Sully, shows a modish Colonial gentleman, learned in the absence of a ritual slaughterer to butcher his own meat in the prescribed traditional manner, though later he trained a young apprentice, Joseph Etting, whose father was one of the first of the Pennsylvania fur traders, to perform the task for him. His brother, Michael, on one of many excursions into Indian territory, carried kosher meat (salted) in his pack train.

It was even harder for those who long preceded my uncle Nathan to San Francisco. During the Gold Rush of 1848, wrote Berg:

> Jewish peddlers in the West who tried to keep the faith found the way of the Torah rockier and more thorny than the trail from Sacramento to Carson City. Isadore Schnayder, when long-awaited pictures of his family arrived on the Sabbath, would not cut the string until nightfall. Abraham Rackovsky sent to Denver for kosher meat, but it spoiled in transit: he turned vegetarian.

But the vast majority of even these hardy souls found "strict Orthodoxy too much to carry on backs already overburdened. Some . . . were lucky enough, in time, to find Christian girls to marry—to which circumstance we owe Barry Goldwater, grandson of Big Mike Goldwasser, peddler and saloon-keeper."

When, as would inevitably happen, these peddlers (among them Levi Strauss, the inventor of jeans) decided to stop traveling and settle down in a particular place, great retail establishments and factories would soon grow up around them. This is why so many department stores all over America have identifiably Jewish names, even if most have long since either come to be owned by descendants who converted to Christianity or been absorbed by larger conglomerates. More astonishing yet, a number of American cities originated as trading posts set up by such peddlers.

One of these, Abraham Mordecai—who, Berg writes, "subscribing to the then popular theory that the Indians were descended from the Ten Lost Tribes," threw off the "yoke" of the Torah, went native, and married an Indian bride—was actually the founding father of Montgomery, Alabama, cradle city of the Southern Confederacy. But another Jewish peddler, Sigmund Schlesinger, evidently rejecting this theory, became so distinguished as an Indian fighter that a barracks-room ballad was written about him: "When the foe charged the breastworks / with the madness of despair, / And the bravest of souls were tested, / the little Jew was there."

M y father also drove a horse and wagon, but it did not belong to him, and even if it had, he could never conceivably have taken it, or himself, even so far out of New York as Long Island or Westchester, never mind some dangerous wilderness in the deep South or the far West. It was as though the trip to America from Galicia had used up all the venturesomeness he had within him. Yet unlike the rest of both sides of his extended family, whose interests (with the exception of a couple of his own brothers) were as bounded as their physical surroundings, he had a mind that *was* able and willing to make forays into the larger world. If his mother-in-law Esther Malkah inhabited one extreme of their almost incredible narrowness of outlook—sheer indifference to and ignorance of what was going on outside the tiny precincts of the immediate family—he was (within certain limits set by the paucity of formal education he had received) at the other.

Almost alone among his elders and his own contemporaries within the family, he kept up with "current events" by diligently reading two newspapers a day, one in Yiddish and one in English. The Yiddish paper he favored was *Der Tog* ("The Day"), which was on a much higher intellectual level than the far more popular daily, *Der Forvertz* ("The Forward"), the vulgarity of whose style, often verging on pidgin-Yiddish, he snobbishly scorned and with whose social-democratic political line he disagreed.

In retrospect, it seems curious to me that my father never bought into the socialism that was so widespread among working-class Jewish immigrants of that era. My guess is that he was on the whole in favor of its domestic program, but I also suspect that its (then) hostility to Zionism overrode any such consideration. Too reclusive ever to join a Zionist organization, he was still an unswerving believer in the need for, and the desirability of, a sovereign Jewish state. On this basis alone, questions of style aside, he would have disliked the *Forvertz*, which (until the state of Israel was actually founded in 1948) had, to put it gently, grave doubts that the "Jewish problem" could be "solved" by political sovereignty, or anything else short of socialism.

It was, I think, also because of Zionism that my father became an anti-Communist. But he was much fiercer in his rejection of Communism than he was in his opposition to socialism. Never do I remember seeing him grow so heated in an argument as he did with the Communist cousin of his brother Joe's wife during a visit to their apartment in Jersey City. I was still a little boy then, and I had no idea what they were quarreling about (was she defending the Nazi-Soviet pact?), but my father's anger—usually under tight wraps—made a great impression on me. When I was older, and my sister, then in her early teens, joined the Communist-front American Youth for Democracy, he constantly berated her for caring more about the fate of the Negroes in America than for her own people, who were, he kept telling her, just then being persecuted to a greater extent in Europe.

Persecuted, yes, and yet for the life of me—odd as it may seem today, when Jews never stop talking about the Holocaust and even in some unlovely sense keep entering it in the perverse competition for recognition as the most victimized of any ethnic or racial group—I cannot recall any mention in our house either before or during the war of the extent of that persecution. But perhaps this was not so odd: it took a long time before even leaders of the Jewish community in America started giving serious credence to the stories that began circulating around 1942 about the death camps.

The English paper my father read every day was the *New York*

Post, which was then earnestly liberal in its editorial line: worship-
ful of Roosevelt and, when the time came, strongly in favor of establishing a Jewish state. It would have amazed and horrified most
American Jews, including my father, to learn that Roosevelt himself, with an eye on the oil fields of Saudi Arabia, would almost
certainly have resisted the creation of Israel had he lived; and they
would have been even more disbelieving had they discovered
while the war was going on that his administration made virtually
no effort to save as many Jews as possible from the fate Hitler had
prepared for them.

But before any of this had come to pass, or come to light, the
Post would have commended itself to my father for its opposition
to the isolationists trying to keep the United States out of the
struggle against Hitler. The most fanatical of these isolationists
were Roosevelt's enemies on the Right. If they were wrong about
his intentions with regard to domestic policy, they were correct in
their belief that the President, while denying it at every step along
the way, was slyly dragging the country toward entering the war
on the side of the British.

Some of these isolationists of the Right were outright Nazi
sympathizers and anti-Semites who thought that Stalin was a
greater threat to us than Hitler; others, like Charles A. Lindbergh
(then still revered as a great hero for having made the first solo
transatlantic flight) and Joseph P. Kennedy (our ambassador to
England and the patriarch of what would eventually become the
most famous political family in America) were pro-German, if not
exactly pro-Nazi. But not all isolationists were on the Right. Norman Thomas, the head of the Socialist party, was (along with
Lindbergh himself) a highly visible member of the most prominent isolationist organization, the America First Committee, and
the leading weekly journal of liberal opinion, *The New Republic,* argued against intervention as well.

On the other hand, it was also on the Left that the most deter-
minedly interventionist group in America could be found, and that

was the Communists during the Popular Front period. However, there was another overnight shift in the Communist line with the signing of the Nazi-Soviet pact in 1939. This previously unthinkable development drove a large contingent out of the party in disgust—the contingent whose support had rested in great part on their conviction that the Soviet Union was the only reliably antifascist power in the world, and that Communism and Nazism were morally and ideologically antithetical. But those who swallowed the pact and, even while gagging all the way, still managed to go on parroting the party line, now joined with the isolationists in calling for America to stay out of the war.

No matter how little may yet have been imagined, or believed, about Hitler's plans for the Jews, enough was known about his anti-Semitism to make it impossible, or so one might have thought, for any Jew to side with the isolationists. But sad to say, there were plenty of Jews who did not see themselves as Jews at all, or who scorned the idea that they had a special obligation to take Jewish interests into consideration in arriving at a political position. For them, Jewish interests were irrelevant or even illegitimate, just as they had been in 1917 to the Polish-Jewish Communist leader Rosa Luxemburg, who once declared that the "special sorrows" of the Jews meant nothing to her, and that she cared far more for the "wretched Indian victims of Putamayo" [!] and "the Negroes in Africa." In the late 1930s, her political and spiritual heirs were driven by much the same ideological considerations into a contemptuous dismissal of "special Jewish sorrows" and they added their voices to the clamor against American entry into the war.

Most of these, like Luxemburg, were Communists, or "Stalinists," as they were by now more commonly called, to differentiate them from members of dissident Communist sects who accused Stalin of having betrayed the ideals of the Russian Revolution. But in opposing intervention, the Stalinists were joined even by some of their worst enemies within the Marxist fold, including a number of anti-Stalinist intellectuals of Jewish origin.* Among the most notable was Clement Greenberg, then one of the editors of the magazine *Partisan Review* and already beginning to achieve the great influence and fame he was destined to acquire as an art critic (for, among many other things, putting Jackson Pollock on the map). Yet even though art was his specialty, Greenberg took the entire world of culture and politics as his domain. Like everyone associated with *Partisan Review*, he never hesitated to make pronouncements on whatever subject he chose that were as self-assured in argument and authoritative in tone as his pieces on contemporary painting.

Thus, in mid-1941, under the influence of the exiled old Bolshevik leader Leon Trotsky, himself a Jew,† Greenberg collaborated with Dwight Macdonald—his colleague on the editorial board of *Partisan Review* and an even more committed Trotskyist—on a piece arguing that fascism could be defeated only by a "social revolution" in England and America that would install "working-class governments" committed to a socialist program. Supporting "the Roosevelt-Churchill war regimes" as "the lesser evil" to Nazi Germany was no way to beat fascism. On the contrary: such a course would either lead to "military defeat owing to

---

*Some of these anti-Stalinist Marxists, including the two I am just about to discuss in more detail, remained opposed to intervention even when, after Hitler's attack on the Soviet Union, the Stalinists joined the war party.

†Trotsky's Jewishness (his real name was Bronstein) brings to mind one of my favorite quotations. Thinking of the anti-Semitism of the Soviet regime which this "non-Jewish Jew," as his equally non-Jewish Jewish biographer Isaac Deutscher would call him, had helped mightily to create when he commanded the Red Army during the Bolshevik takeover of Russia in 1917, the chief rabbi of Moscow once commented drily: "The Trotskys make the revolution, the Bronsteins pay the bill." Ironically, one of the Bronsteins who paid the bill, though not on account of his Jewishness, was Trotsky himself, first driven into exile and then murdered by a hit man sent to his sanctuary in Mexico on Stalin's orders.

the superiority of fascism in total warfare; or victory under a fascist system of our own" that the exigencies of war would create. Neither in the "Ten Propositions on the War" in which they developed this position, nor in their follow-up answer to criticisms of it, did the word "Jew" appear even once.

Then too there were Jewish intellectuals like Paul Goodman, who was then on the outs with the *Partisan Review* crowd and who would become (with, I now blush with embarrassment to confess, more than a little push from me) one of the great gurus of the youth culture of the 1960s. A social critic, novelist, poet, and philosopher all wrapped into one, Goodman was also a pacifist, and it was on this ground that he opposed American entry into the war.

Whenever I think about these people and their arguments, so charged with intellectual firepower and the special erudition that intra-Marxist polemics required and elicited, I am inevitably reminded of another of my favorite quotations, this one from the then not very well known British writer George Orwell. Having himself taken a brief plunge into Trotskyism before the war actually broke out, Orwell experienced a radical change of heart when it did, becoming so passionate a patriot as to write an article entitled "My Country, Left or Right." It was in this mood that he exploded in commenting on a number of analyses of the war's progress (the most prominent of which was almost exactly the same as the Greenberg-Macdonald thesis that there could be no victory without a prior social revolution): "One has to belong to the intelligentsia to believe things like that; no ordinary man could be such a fool."

A homelier version of the same attitude toward intellectuals once came from the aunt of Saul Bellow, who remarked after listening to the future Nobel laureate for literature and a group of his fellow undergraduate radicals at the University of Chicago engage in a raucous ideological discussion in her nearby apartment: "Smart, smart, smart. . . . Stupid." Similarly, my own mother, who normally paid the humblest deference to anyone with advanced college degrees, once declared in exasperation at something she heard some professor say on television, "For *that* you need a Ph.D.?" She also said of the husband of one of her nieces, who had announced that he was leaving his wife just as she had given birth to twins (and to whom without fail my mother referred ever after as "Harvey-he-should-drop-dead"): "Only someone with a Ph.D. could do a thing like that."

Fortunately for the honor of the American intellectual class, there were enough members of it who were neither such fools nor so cruel. For example, William Phillips and Philip Rahv, the two chief editors of *Partisan Review* (both of whom were Jewish), took strong exception to the Greenberg-Macdonald piece. To be sure, until the United States entered the war, their own mildly Trotsky-ist leanings held them back from wholehearted support of inter-vention (in a rebuttal entitled "Ten Propositions and Eight Errors"—in which, incidentally, the word "Jew" again never ap-peared—Rahv wrote: "In a sense, this war, even if it accomplishes the destruction of fascism, is not yet *our* war"*). But the differences on this issue were sharp enough to cause what Macdonald would describe in a memoir as a series of "first-class rows," and both he and Greenberg eventually left the magazine.

---

*I hardly need to add—but it may be worth emphasizing anyway—that the "our" here meant "we anti-Stalinist Marxists" and not "we Jews." As I have discov-ered upon rereading all these by-now ancient polemics, even when the war against Hitler became "our" war for the Jews in this group, it was still not because "we" as Jews had a special stake in his defeat. It was because "we" as Marxists, or even (a new idea, just beginning to take root) "we" as Americans, had concluded that the "bourgeois democracies" really could do the job of defeating fascism without ben-efit of a prior socialist revolution. An even more shockingly new idea that just had started to penetrate these Marxist skulls, much to Dwight Macdonald's disgust (though he too came around on this particular point in the decade ahead), was that the bourgeois democracies were perhaps something better than a mere "lesser evil" as compared with Nazism.

Neither Macdonald nor Goodman ever changed his mind about the war, though Greenberg certainly did, and once the United States had been drawn in by the attack on Pearl Harbor, Rahv and Phillips finally acknowledged it without qualification as "our war." So did Mary McCarthy—yet another brilliant intellectual associated with *Partisan Review* who, unlike Greenberg but like Macdonald, at least had the excuse, so to speak, of not being Jewish when she had endorsed their position. But one morning after the United States had entered the fray, she awoke to the startled realization that this was "our war" after all and that she wanted America to win. Decades later, during the Vietnam war, she would go to the other extreme, and proclaim to all the world that she wanted America to lose.* But in 1947, early in the long interval between these two events, she wrote an essay for *Commentary* entitled "America the Beautiful." That there was at least some degree of sarcasm in this title became clear from her statement that "nearly everything that is beautiful [in America] and has not been produced by nature belongs to the eighteenth century." Nonetheless, she stated flat out that she "admired and liked" this country, and she set about to defend it against the standard European charge that its people cared about nothing but money. (The opposite, she

---

*It is instructive to compare Mary McCarthy's attitude toward the Vietnam war with that of Bertrand Russell during the First World War. Russell was vehemently opposed to that war, and even went to jail for agitating against conscription. Yet he could write: "In the midst of this, I was myself tortured by patriotism. The successes of the Germans at the Marne were horrible to me. I desired the defeat of Germany as ardently as any retired colonel." Of course, as a very old man, Russell himself took the same position about Vietnam as Mary McCarthy did, even to the extent of serving as a judge in a show trial designed to demonstrate that America was committing war crimes. But America was not Russell's country, and he had long borne a grudge against it. As to those alleged war crimes, incidentally, Guenter Lewy has shown conclusively in his *America in Vietnam*, and I myself have set forth additional evidence in *Why We Were in Vietnam*, that the charges made, and sustained, by the tribunal were all false.

declared with the contrarian bravado so typical of her work in that period, was true: "The virtue of American civilization is that it is unmaterialistic.") In thus defending America, she was as lacking in sarcasm as it was possible for "our leading bitch intellectual" to be (except, that is, in her sycophantic portraits of the North Vietnamese Communist leaders whom she met on a visit to Hanoi in 1967).

B̲ut to return to the years immediately preceding American entry into the war, the change in the Communist (or Stalinist) line from pro- to anti-intervention after the signing of the Hitler-Stalin pact might logically have been expected to bring with it a corresponding change in the patriotic dances choreographed by the Popular Front. Nothing of the kind: like the America Firsters, the Communists opposed intervention in the name of American interests, complete with citations from George Washington and Thomas Jefferson about avoiding foreign entanglements. This meant that the atmosphere in which I spent the rest of my preteen years was just as charged with patriotic sentiment (both real and feigned) as it had been earlier. There were patriots to the Right of me, and patriots to the Left of me, and even without fully grasping what they were talking about or why or what was actually behind the clamor, I have no doubt that I was affected by this atmosphere as it filtered down through teachers, radio programs, and the movies.

I was just about a month shy of my twelfth birthday when the Japanese attacked Pearl Harbor, and I sat enthralled with my parents and my sister around that big Zenith console radio in our living room listening to the dulcet voice of President Roosevelt, suddenly imbued with a gravity that contrasted dramatically with its customary cheerfulness, announce that December 7, 1941, was "a date that shall live in infamy." Within the next few days, we were at war both with the Japanese themselves and also with their allies, Hitler's Germany and the Italy of Mussolini. Now the British—whose gallantry had been brought home even to an eleven-year-old like me through the on-the-spot radio broadcasts from London of Edward R. Murrow and through newsreels of the nightly bombardment of that city—would have us with them in the lonely stand they had mounted against the Nazis after the conquest and occupation of France in 1940.

Furthermore, since Hitler, in violation of his pact with Stalin, had invaded the Soviet Union only a few months earlier, the Communist line flipped cavalierly once again from isolationist to interventionist. In line with this change, the spirit of the Popular Front was resurrected, and it came roaring back in the much more serious form of a wartime alliance.

In recounting this history, I have had to do a bit of research, but I have also been trying very hard to include mainly those details that I myself either knew or was vaguely conscious of through (to borrow a phrase from another context) their penumbras and emanations. After sixty years, however, I cannot honestly tell how much I took in then. Obviously some of the events and disputes I have been describing (those, for instance, that occurred on the editorial board of *Partisan Review*), I could only have learned about later. And even there, in checking for accuracy, I have discovered that my memory was faulty or incomplete. What I can be sure of, however, is how thrilling it felt to be at war on the side of good against the forces of evil.

Among the details I most assuredly did not know at the time was that our new ally Stalin was as much a force for evil as his new enemy Hitler. Winston Churchill knew, but I had no idea that the great British leader—who in my eyes was up there on Mount Olympus with Roosevelt himself—had, in justifying the alliance with Stalin, said that he would make a deal with the devil in order to defeat the Nazis. I did not even know that Churchill was the

British equivalent of a Republican and not a liberal like Roosevelt. I did not know that the British novelist Evelyn Waugh, another Tory (though "reactionary"—an epithet hurled promiscuously by the Left against anyone who disagreed with it—would in this unusual instance for once have been accurate), had actually rejoiced upon hearing of the Hitler-Stalin pact because "The enemy at last was plain in view, huge and hateful, all disguise cast off. It was the Modern Age in arms." By bringing together the two great contemporary threats to civilization, and revealing that they were in actual fact one, the pact had given Waugh an incentive to fight. As he said of Guy Crouchback, his protagonist in *Men at Arms, Officers and Gentlemen,* and *The End of the Battle,* the great trilogy of novels he wrote after the war itself had ended: "Whatever the outcome there was a place for him in that battle." Conversely, "the just cause of going to war" had then "been forfeited in the Russian alliance" with England. With that alliance, the illusion "was dissolved" and England had been "led blundering into dishonor," so that only "personal honor" was left to be salvaged.

But I had not yet ever heard of Waugh, and I only came upon these sentiments when he put them into Guy Crouchback's mouth. By the time I read the trilogy, I understood exactly what Waugh meant and I agreed with him about the kinship between Nazi Germany and Soviet Russia. Where I disagreed was on the identity of the enemy: to me, it was not the Modern Age in general but more specifically the great curse of the Modern Age, totalitarianism. I also remained convinced that from a prudential point of view Churchill had been right in joining with Stalin to defeat Hitler, and that he had in no manner, shape, or form led his country into dishonor by making that alliance. But even setting these two great reservations aside, if, while the war was going on, I had heard such a thing as Waugh gave Guy Crouchback to say, I would have found it incomprehensible; or, if comprehensible, demented in equating Nazi Germany with the Soviet Union, and perhaps even evil in itself.

For in spite of the fact that I also did not know—and it was the biggest of all the things I (along with practically everyone else) did not know—that Hitler seriously intended to murder all the Jews of Europe, I (and everyone else) did know perfectly well that he was a great enemy of the Jewish people. He had long since begun passing laws against the Jews of his own country, and he was rounding up those of Poland, France, and the other countries he had already conquered and sending them to special prisons called concentration camps.

Yet not even as relentless an anti-Communist as my father imagined that anything remotely comparable could happen in the Soviet Union. That anti-Semitism still existed there, despite claims to the contrary; that Jewish writers and actors had been arrested, never to appear again; that the rich Yiddish culture created over the centuries by Russian Jewry had either been wiped out or been allowed to remain alive only to the extent that it served as an instrument of Communist propaganda; and that the practice of the Jewish religion had for all practical purposes been outlawed—all this had been reported in the Yiddish paper in America that my father pored over so thoroughly (while these truths were simultaneously being denounced as libelous by the Yiddish Communist daily, the *Freiheit*).

But bad as conditions were for the Jews in the Soviet Union, they still did not compare with what Hitler was doing; and if I had ever discussed the matter with my father, I have no doubt that, notwithstanding his hatred of Communism and his fury at the treatment of Jews living under it, he would have agreed with Churchill about the practical value of an alliance with Stalin and the justification for joining with the lesser evil against the greater.

I needed no such justification. So far as I was concerned, the only word for the Soviet Union was heroic, and my admiration for the struggle its people were putting up against the invading Nazi hordes knew no bounds. This admiration erupted into the most ambitious literary effort I had ever made: a very long poem, written in blank verse (or some approximation of it), about the Battle of Stalingrad that was entitled (what else?) "Stalingrad." I was twelve years old when, in August 1942, this epic battle began and just a month past my bar-mitzvah when what at first had looked like an inevitable Germany victory, which would lead inexorably to the conquest of Russia, ended with the opposite result. House to house the two armies fought, with the Russians (in the words of one historian) "contest[ing] every street and factory, whether still standing or totally destroyed. Territory which the Germans, with their superior fire power, had won by day was regained by night." By November the Russians had managed to pour in enough reinforcements to encircle the invaders, and "the besiegers were besieged." Hitler himself, as I have since discovered, was disgusted when in February 1943 his commanding general defied him by surrendering instead of committing suicide, and he was also dismayed. "The god of war," he said, "has gone over to the other side."

"Stalingrad" was my own contribution to the hosannahs that were being sung all over America and that wiped out all remaining traces of disgust with Stalin—after whom that now glorious city had been named—for having made a pact with Hitler four years earlier. I am happy to report that there are no surviving copies of this juvenile effusion of mine, about which I remember nothing except that it was endless. It must also have been a precocious specimen of the kind of "agitation and propaganda" (or "agitprop" for short) that Communist writers had a duty to produce, since it elicited great admiration from a history teacher I had in high school (who, as I later realized, was a member of the party) and then from the editor of the magazine published by the American Youth for Democracy to whom he sent me with it.

But stirred as I was by this great feat of the Russian army, my wartime passions were mainly aroused by and focused on our own "boys" and the feats of arms *they* performed after a shaky start. There was the pilot Captain Colin Kelly, who became our first hero when in the earliest days of the war he attacked a Japanese heavy cruiser, and shortly thereafter was killed when his plane crashed into a mountain: President Roosevelt himself went on the air to promise that a special scholarship would be set up at West Point for his little son. On a more exalted level, there was General Douglas MacArthur vowing as he was driven out of the Philippines, "I shall return." There was the Battle of Midway, a kind of seagoing Stalingrad of our own, that turned the tide of the naval war in the Pacific and became our revenge for Pearl Harbor. There was the much-decorated Audie Murphy, who won the Congressional Medal of Honor for single-handedly taking on a whole company of German infantry while standing on top of a tank that might have exploded at any minute, and still surviving to tell the tale.

Added to these real-life thrills were the movies about American fighting men on land, on sea, and in the air: the same breed of ordinary Joes who populated the world of the Frank Capras and who, now in uniform, went through vividly depicted hardships, griping constantly in the good-old-fashioned American way but, when it came to it, standing up to the evil Nazis on one front and the vicious "Japs" on the other, always doing what they had to do, also in the good-old-fashioned American way.

Naturally, the horrors of the war were never so vividly shown as they would be many years later by Steven Spielberg in *Saving Private Ryan:* this would have been offputting and might have defeated the purpose of keeping up the morale of "the home front." And the home front was all-important. "They also serve who only stand and wait," wrote John Milton in the seventeenth century, but that was of a very different kind of war. In this one, the women did not stand and wait, they worked. "Rosie the Riveter" replaced her husband or boyfriend at the factories turning out unprecedented quantities of war materiel. Other women did their bit through various forms of volunteer activity, while kids like me collected silver foil from cigarette packs and rolled them into great balls to be recycled into . . . what? bullets?; we also saved up our dimes for stamps that slowly grew into $25 war bonds.

As we saved, we listened and learned to dance to war songs with lyrics like "Praise the Lord and pass the ammunition" and romantic ballads about the pains of separation that the girls back home felt for their boyfriends overseas and the promises made and sometimes broken between them ("Don't sit under the apple tree with anyone else but me / Till I come marching home"; "I left my heart at the Stage-Door Canteen"; "Saturday night is the loneliest night of the week"; and a hundred others that have disappeared into whatever graveyard sentimental songs go to die).

Most of all, we wished that we were old enough to join one of the services and do some fighting ourselves. I had no big brother to envy, but most of the older guys on the block wound up in uniform—except for the few who suffered the shame of being classified "4-F," which meant that they were rejected as physically unfit ("What's good is in the army, / What's left will never harm me," crooned Kitty Kallen with Jimmy Dorsey's band behind her). A dozen or more of my cousins also went into the army. Before the war ended, I would in addition have a brother-in-law in the Air Corps and two uncles (one of them the son Esther Malkah grieved over when he was drafted and the other—was there no limit to her afflictions?—the husband of her youngest daughter).

Not all these relatives or neighbors were sent into combat, but of those who were, not a single one was either killed or wounded. Which, of course, helped bolster the romantic fantasies I entertained about going to war and giving my all for "the land of the brave and the free." As with the popular songs that filled the airwaves during the war years, I memorized, and often enthusiastically sang, every word of every anthem of every branch of every military service, from the familiar "Anchors Aweigh" of the Navy and the Marines' "From the halls of Montezuma to the shores of

Tripoli" (wherever they were), to the less familiar "Over hill, over dale, we will hit the dusty trail, as those caissons [whatever *they* were] go rolling along," and to the newer Air Corps' "Off we go into the wild blue yonder" (which ended with the wonderfully bravado lines, "We live in fame or go down in flame / Nothing can stop the Army Air Corps"). To be allowed to join up and don any one of the uniforms that went with those songs would have been very heaven to me.

For never in my young life had I ever felt so pure a love for anything or anyone as I did for America during the war. In my eyes, we stood for everything good and noble, and if ever a word was spoken to contradict that idea, I never heard it. The isolationists on the Right and on the Left had been silenced by Pearl Harbor, and many of them rushed to enlist (including Lindbergh, who went on to fly combat missions in the Pacific). As for those whose opposition to intervention had been based on pacifist principles, they either submitted uncomplainingly to jail as "conscientious objectors" or volunteered for various projects through which even they could contribute to the war effort without being asked to kill.

In such an atmosphere, there was only reinforcement for my love of America, and nothing and no one to question or plant doubts about it in my head. With so much nourishment, it struck deep roots in my soul and in my mind that would remain planted there and blossom anew even in another and much less hospitable climate. An analogous process was set into motion by the romantic idea of the military that World War Two planted within me. When the war ended, I was still only fifteen years old, and along with the jubilation first of V-E Day, when the Germans surrendered, and then of V-J Day, when it was the turn of the Japanese (who would have gone on fighting much longer if not for the atomic bombs we had dropped on two of their cities), I experienced a touch of regret. Now I would never get a chance to find out what it was like to be a soldier fighting for my country and whether I was man enough to take it.

This feeling too stayed with me in so powerful a condition that it eventually demanded satisfaction even when I might easily have denied it any. Fast-forwarding yet again, I see myself five years later, in September 1950, standing on the deck of an ocean liner bound for England. Having just been chosen by Columbia to be that year's Kellett Fellow at Clare College, Cambridge, my cup is now, not just running, but pouring over from the addition of one of the Fulbright scholarships that Congress recently established with the same purpose of sending American students to universities abroad. Because (unlike the Kellett) the U.S. government includes transportation as part of its generous package, I am traveling not with Ida Chill's son but with all the other Fulbrights en route to various universities in Europe.

As the ship sets sail, we are all talking about the war which has just broken out in Korea and how it might affect us, when a charmingly roguish character from New Mexico with a blond mustache comes up with a pungent expression of the general mood: "I don't mind *di*arrhea, and I don't mind *pyo*rrhea, but I don't want none of that *Ko*rea." I laugh along with everyone else, but unlike everyone else's, mine is an uneasy laugh. Certainly I would not wish to be drafted now, just when I am about to be launched on a great adventure of another kind. Not that there is any danger of being drafted: as a student, I enjoy an exemption, and unless the rules should change, I will continue to be exempt for the three years at Cambridge that my two fellowships together have given me, and as many after that as it takes for me to complete the Ph.D. I am planning to get. By then the war will surely be over anyway.

Yet fast-forwarding once more to the spring of 1953 and the end of my third year in Cambridge, I hear myself turning down that offer from Clare to stay on there as a teaching fellow. With a sheepishness bred of my newly sophisticated awareness of how naïve I must sound to anyone who has been through military service and harbors no illusions about it, I explain that I have decided to go home and make myself available to the draft. Sheepish or not, the yearning to be in uniform that I had felt as a kid is still there, and because of it I for one *do* want some of "that *Ko*rea." But only in all truth some, which is why I would rather be drafted than volunteer. A draftee is only required to serve two years on active duty (with six thereafter in the reserves), whereas the minimum term for a volunteer is three. Two is enough for me, especially when at least one of them is likely to be spent in combat.

In the late spring of 1953, then, with the war still raging, back I go to the United States and present myself to the draft board. Even the members of that board can hardly believe their ears when I tell them my story: they too obviously think I am either crazy or—considering how much education I have had—unaccountably innocent. Perhaps that is why they take nearly six months before calling me up, by which point an armistice has been signed. When I am inducted into the army in December, then, there is no longer any prospect that I will wind up in combat. I am a little disappointed, but also, and again sheepishly, relieved at having gotten it both ways: becoming a soldier but spared the risks of actually having to fight and maybe even being killed.

I have a friend, ten years my senior, who was also born in a Brooklyn slum of working-class Jewish immigrants and who then went on to the largely Jewish CCNY of the 1930s, where he spent most of his days reading and arguing about Marx. Once he told me that being in the army during World War Two had exposed him for the first time to Americans who were neither Jewish nor in the least interested in ideas, and especially not the ideas that to him had contained the answers to every question there was about the world in general and America in particular. It was a shocking and liberating experience that had a lasting influence on his thinking about the nature of this country.

As I will explain in greater detail a little later on, something similar happened to me during my two years as a soldier. But in my case the shock was less jolting than it had been to him. Because I had gone not to CCNY but to Columbia, where the vast majority of the student body was not Jewish and was drawn from all over the United States, and because I had never really been much of a Marxist in the first place, I had already learned that there were more things in heaven and earth than were dreamt of in the philosophy of Brooklyn or the left-liberal politics of the Popular Front on which I had cut my teeth. (Some of my classmates were even, *mirabile dictu*, Republicans.)

Nevertheless, the America I loved was still mainly an abstraction, and not until the summers of 1949 and 1950, when I worked as a counselor at a camp in northern Wisconsin, did I begin to get a glimpse of how life was lived in other places and in other classes of society.

Once, on my day off from the camp, I went with another counselor to visit his parents who had a vacation retreat fifty miles or so away. When we started out, the day was sunny, but as we were standing on a highway trying to hitch a ride there was a sudden downpour, and we were both soaked to the skin when we finally arrived at our destination, which turned out to be what in my inexperienced eyes was a very grand lakefront house. My friend's mother naturally insisted that we get into some dry clothes, and she sent me up to a room where, she said, I would find what I needed.

Already awed by the size and luxuriousness of this house, the like of which I had never seen at such close quarters or from within, I made my dazzled way up the stairs and entered the room—one of many up there—to which she had directed me. The door was open, and when I closed it, there was a click as the latch snapped firmly into place. At the sound of this click, I burst into tears. Bewildered by my strange reaction, I stood there weeping for a few seconds, and then it came to me that what had caused it was the fact that the doors in our apartment in Brooklyn, thickly encrusted as they had become from repeated painting over the years, could never be snapped shut with that marvelously satisfying click. I was nineteen years old, and I had been inside a few luxurious apartments when visiting Columbia classmates in Manhattan. Yet it took this trivial detail to make me realize fully for the first time in my life that I was *poor*, that I had never had a room all to myself until a short while ago, and that when I finally got one, I could never even close the door for complete privacy.

In telling this story, I am very uncomfortably conscious of opening myself to the charge made by an acerbic critic against *Awake and Sing*, the once celebrated play by Clifford Odets about a Jewish family in the Bronx during the Depression. "I wish," said this critic, "that Odets would stop whining about how he never had a bicycle when he was a kid." Now I am about to make things worse by going on to reveal that I wept even more bitterly when I slid open the rustically unpainted knotty-pine doors of the closet and was assailed by the sight of stacks of gleaming white underwear neatly piled on one shelf, a dozen or so pairs of socks and handkerchiefs on another, and polo shirts galore resting on hangers above them.

There was, of course, a large dose of self-pity in those tears, but not, I feel sure, any envy. I did not, then or in later life, aspire to wealth or the things large sums of money could buy. (Fame was what I wanted.) But when I closed that door and heard the sound of that click, vistas of previously undreamed-of possibility invaded my imagination. That I, coming from where I came and growing up under the circumstances in which I had grown up, had been given the chance to go to a college like Columbia (and then, though I had not yet been apprised of this, on to a university like Cambridge) proved in itself that America was indeed a "land of opportunity." But as I stood, tears streaming down my face and my body wracked with sobs, in an opulently appointed summer home in the gorgeous north woods of Wisconsin, the revelation came to me that until now I had not yet so much as begun to know the half of what America was all about, and what it might have to offer, even for the likes of me. My native land was by now less of an abstraction than it had been before, but an abstraction it still largely was.

Before long, however, it would turn from an abstraction into an issue. No sooner was I, to my delighted amazement (who had expected anything like this?), settled into a two-room suite in the newer part of Clare College with a servant attached (and whose doors I had no trouble snapping shut) than I found myself being dragged into arguments about America by the students around me at Cambridge. The Korean war was in full bloody swing, and congressional investigations (all summed up under the rubric of "McCarthyism," though Senator McCarthy's committee was only one of several such) were being conducted both of Communist espionage within the government and Communist influence in various institutions of American society. For all this, I (like every other American in Europe in those days) was called to account, and had to endure a constant barrage of challenges and even insults.

These insults were probably most vicious in France, which had one of the two largest Communist parties in Western Europe (the other was in Italy), but they could also be very nasty at Cambridge. Everyone I ran into there seemed to be either a Communist (not for nothing had Cambridge been the breeding-ground of the Soviet spy ring in the 1930s that had included Anthony Blunt and Guy Burgess) or a "neutralist" of the Left who (shades of the old theory of "social fascism" in reverse) could perceive no differences between the Soviet Union and the United States worth fighting about.

And indeed, the Communists and their sympathizers all interpreted McCarthyism as a sign that America was on the road to fascism, if it had not already arrived there; many of them bought the unsubstantiated and later altogether discredited charge (originating with the Communists but more widely disseminated by the then highly influential socialist weekly, *The New Statesman*) that the United States was engaging in germ warfare in Korea; and hardly a one doubted that its "fanatical" crusade against Communism would sooner or later drag the world into a nuclear holocaust.

Yet not even anti-Communists like the poet and critic Stephen Spender were willing to leap to the defense of America. Thus, in his contribution to *The God That Failed*, a newly (1950) published volume of six personal accounts by ex-Communists of why they had become disillusioned with a cause they had once embraced with a veritable religious intensity, Spender felt it necessary to include a cautious disclaimer:

> In writing this essay, I have always been aware that no criticism of the Communists removes the arguments against capitalism. The effect of these years of painful experiences has only been to reveal to me that both sides are forces producing oppression, injustice, destruction of liberties, enormous evils.

Or again: "America, the greatest capitalist country, seems to offer no alternative to war, exploitation and destruction of the world's resources."

More significantly, not even another of the contributors to *The God That Failed*, Arthur Koestler, whose novel *Darkness at Noon* was one of the most important exposés yet written of the true nature of Communism, could bring himself to judge as anything better than the lesser of two evils the country that was expending so much treasure and blood in the battle against this horrific force. "The choice before us," he once astonishingly said of the cold war, "is merely that between a grey twilight and total darkness."

Nor did the minority on the Right at Cambridge have a good

word for America. A large number of them saw nothing implausible in the political charges made by the Left, but they seemed in their flippant way more horrified by the prospect of being drowned by Coca-Cola and poisoned by hamburgers than incinerated by nuclear bombs. It was an attitude encapsulated in the much-quoted crack that Georges Clemenceau had supposedly made as prime minister of France during the negotiations at Versailles after the end of World War One: "America is the only nation in history which miraculously has gone from barbarism to degeneration without the usual interval of civilization."* So far as the right-wing lovers of this quotation were concerned, America had since then sunk even deeper into decadence. While risibly claiming to be the defender of Western civilization, it was itself a mortal threat to that civilization, and a far greater one than the Soviet Union.

As a liberal who was also developing into a bit of a cultural snob, I might have gone along with these two sets of charges against America, just as plenty of other American students in Europe did. At Cambridge, to cite only the most egregious example, one of my fellow Fulbright scholars, who never bothered to conceal his membership in the Communist party, used a portion of the grant he had received from the American government to buy a mimeograph machine on which he printed diatribes against that very government similar to those emanating from the English Left.

One might have thought that the mere presence of such a person engaged in such activities while being supported by the American government would have introduced a little complexity into the picture of America as a country caught up in a frenzy of anti-Communist "witch hunts." If that were a true picture, how had so frank and open a "witch" been awarded a government grant to

---

*Another version or translation of the same crack has it as "decadence" rather than "degeneration."

study abroad, and how was it possible for him to be doing what he was doing without concealment and yet without being denounced to the authorities?

For that matter (jumping ahead a bit), how could this politically garish picture of America be reconciled with the willingness of the Congress for Cultural Freedom—an organization later revealed to have been secretly funded by the CIA—to hire Stephen Spender as co-editor of *Encounter,* one of the many magazines it would establish in various countries with the express purpose of trying to counter the influence of the Communists on the intellectuals? Even under the highly doubtful assumption that Spender was telling the truth when he would later claim not to have known that he was being paid by the CIA, we would still be left with the question of why the CIA was willing to pay *him* in spite of the neutralist stance he took in *The God That Failed* and elsewhere.

In 1967, when the CIA's sponsorship of the Congress for Cultural Freedom would be exposed, the debates triggered by the resulting scandal would provide an answer to this question. The idea behind the entire project, it would then be said by its defenders (who did not include Spender himself: he went around expressing—or, as I believe, feigning—outrage at having been duped), was that the most effective way of conducting the "cultural cold war" was to enlist anti- and ex-Communist intellectuals who had broken with the party on the ground that under Stalin it had betrayed the ideals of the Left, to which they themselves remained loyal, either as democratic socialists or liberals. (Anti-Communists like Whittaker Chambers or Max Eastman or James Burnham, who had moved all the way from Communism, either of the Stalinist or the Trotskyist variety, to the Right had, it was not unreasonably thought, lost their "credibility" with other intellectuals.)

Yet the stark fact remains that if America in the early 1950s had really been an incipiently fascist state crazed by paranoid delusions about the Soviet Union, searching for "a Communist under every bed," and unable to tell the difference between a Communist and a liberal, let alone a socialist, the CIA would never have trusted, still less put on its payroll, people to whom "both sides" in the cold war were "forces producing oppression, injustice, destruction of liberties, enormous evils."

But at the time no such complicating consideration about the state of affairs in America ever seemed to enter anyone's mind, and whenever I tried to put it there, I invariably failed. The reason I tried was not that I supported McCarthy or McCarthyism. Like all liberals, I was against the methods being employed by the congressional committees and embarrassed by them. Even as the anti-Communist I had now become under the tutelage of Lionel Trilling, Hannah Arendt, and a number of other writers who had convinced me that Communism was no less evil than Nazism, and that the fight against it was as urgent a moral and political duty as the fight against Hitler had been, I thought that the only achievement of McCarthyism was to bring discredit on this fight and to make it seem disreputable.

Unbeknownst to me in the early 1950s, Whittaker Chambers took exactly this view in cautioning his young friend William F. Buckley, Jr. against becoming an apologist for McCarthy. Buckley revered Chambers for his heroic willingness to ruin himself by exposing Alger Hiss as a Soviet agent—and he also thought, as I too did and do—that Chambers's autobiography *Witness* was a great book. But he did not take the older man's advice on the issue of McCarthy, to whose defense he sprang. In 1999, however, ten years after the fall of Communism, Buckley would publish a fascinating novel about McCarthy, *The Redhunter,* that would go some distance toward the position Chambers had urged him to take in the 1950s.

Quite apart from the idea prevalent around me at Cambridge of McCarthy's power, which I considered (rightly, as was shown by the ease with which he would be toppled in 1954 after a

run in the spotlight that had lasted only four years) almost de-
mentedly exaggerated, I did not recognize my own country in the
denunciations of it that kept coming at me from all sides. Granted,
even by this point in my life I still had seen relatively little of
America and I still had much to learn about what it was like outside
the relatively narrow confines with which I had become familiar.
Yet that was a lot more than could be claimed by the Englishmen
or other Europeans who were so confidently characterizing the
country in such overheated and bigoted terms. If I was provincial
with respect to what non–New Yorkers were pleased to call the
"real" America, few of these Europeans had ever even set foot anywhere in the place.

I have already said that living abroad made me realize how
American I was and that even the two countries in which I might
have felt completely at home—England because I loved its language and was steeped in its literature, and Israel because I was a
Jew with a strong sense of my connection to the Jewish past—began to seem more and more foreign to me the longer I stayed in
them. But the anti-Americanism I encountered everywhere I went
did more than strengthen my deepening recognition that America
was my true home; it also resurrected the patriotic zeal that I had
grown up with as a child. The difference was that now, in its new
incarnation, my patriotism took the form not of a vaguely exalted
sentiment but of a clearly defined political position. Which is to
say that in response to the anti-American passions befouling the
European atmosphere, I became positively *pro*-American, and I
could back up this partisanship with arguments that made my opponents froth at the mouth but were not all that easy for them to
counter or dismiss.

Whenever America was attacked in my presence, I defended it
with commensurate vigor first for having only a few short years
earlier thrown its all into helping defeat one form of totalitarianism and now for doing the same to hold the line against the other.

Nor did I restrict myself to the political realm. I also took equally vigorous issue with the Clemenceau line about the country's culture. In doing so, I leaned on several recent books, one of the most helpful being David Riesman's *The Lonely Crowd* (written in collaboration with Nathan Glazer and Reuel Denney). Though critical of certain aspects and tendencies of American society, Riesman took a much more positive look at it as a living and developing organism than previous sociologists working in the dyspeptic spirit of Thorstein Veblen had ever done. He even was audacious enough to venture the opinion that America might be producing "one of the great cultures of history."

Additional reinforcements even came from a few European works, both old and new. Of the old, the best by far was Alexis de Tocqueville's *Democracy in America*. This great work, long neglected, had now been rediscovered, and so profound was its account of the features and contours—many of them good, some of them bad—of a revolutionary new system based on "equality of condition," as against the old "distinctions of rank" and social class, that it seemed scarcely dated more than a century after its original publication.*

As if all that were not enough, Tocqueville's first volume concluded with the following passage, which to the eyes of anyone reading it during the cold war—myself most emphatically included—was bound to seem uncannily prophetic:

> There are at the present time two great nations in the world, . . . the Russians and the Americans. . . . [W]hile the atten-

---

*Given that Tocqueville was now being quoted so often that someone—I forget who—could jokingly brag that he had written a whole book about America without referring to *Democracy in America* even once, I am still amazed when I recall that it was out of print in English translation and hard to find for forty whole years before a new edition was brought out in 1945.

tion of mankind was directed elsewhere, they have suddenly placed themselves in the front rank among the nations. . . . The American struggles against the obstacles that nature opposes to him; the adversaries of the Russians are men. The former combats the wilderness and savage life; the latter, civilization with all its arms. The conquests of the American are therefore gained by the plowshare; those of the Russians by the sword. The Anglo-American relies upon personal interest to accomplish his ends and gives free scope to the unguided strength and common sense of the people; the Russian centers all the authority of society in a single arm. The principal instrument of the former is freedom; of the latter servitude. Their starting-point is different and their courses are not the same; yet each of them seems marked out by the will of Heaven to sway the destinies of half the globe.

Of the new European books that proved useful and encouraging to me in combating anti-Americanism, the ones I liked most were those by the historian D. W. Brogan. Himself a professor at Cambridge whose scholarly specialty was France, he was highly unusual among the British academics of his day in considering America "the most interesting country in the world": there was, he said, no parallel in history "to the experiment of free government" on so large a scale that had been undertaken in the United States. Brogan was a latter-day Tocqueville, and while his work was not on the same level of greatness (whose was?), its analyses of the American polity and of American society tacitly demonstrated in great and persuasive detail why an attitude like Clemenceau's was a piece of rank philistinism and itself guilty of the decadence it attributed to the United States.

I am reminded here again of Henry Adams. The direct descendant of two American Presidents (John Adams was his great-grandfather and John Quincy Adams his grandfather), this brilliant and bitter writer, historian, and intellectual took to blaming the rampant capitalism of the "Gilded Age" in which he lived most of his adult life for having plunged America into a steep political, cultural, and moral decline. In thus ranting against the materialism, corruption, and philistinism that the new industrialists of the period after the Civil War had brought with them, Adams conveniently forgot that eminent foreigners, including the great English poet William Wordsworth, had made almost exactly the same charges against the *pre*-industrial and *pre*-capitalist America of 1800. Adams also forgot that he himself had written one of the most eloquent answers to those charges:

> In the foreigner's range of observation, love of money was the most conspicuous and most common trait of the American character. . . . No foreigner of that day—neither poet, painter, nor philosopher—could detect in American life anything higher than vulgarity. . . . Englishmen especially indulged in unbounded invective against the sordid character of American society. . . . Contemporary critics could see neither generosity, economy, honor, nor ideas of any kind in the American breast. . . . [Even Wordsworth] could do no better, when he stood in the face of American democracy, than "keep the secret of a poignant scorn."

Yet, Adams went on,

> Wordsworth might have convinced himself by a moment's thought that no country could act on the imagination as America acted upon the instincts of the ignorant and poor, without some quality that deserved better treatment than poignant scorn.

Indeed, he continued, while the philosophers and the poets could see only rapacity and vulgarity in America, "the poorest peasant in Europe" could discern "the dim outline of a mountain-summit across the ocean, rising high above the mist and mud of American democracy." What the poor peasant discerned, said Adams, was that

> . . . the hard, practical money-getting American democrat, who had neither generosity nor honor nor imagination, and who inhabited cold shades where fancy sickened and where genius died, was in truth living in a world of dream, and acting a drama more instinct with poetry than all the avatars of the east, walking in gardens of emerald and rubies, in ambition already ruling the world and guiding Nature with a kinder and wiser hand than had ever yet been felt in human history.

It was to these poor European peasants that the "American speculator" of 1800 beckoned, inviting them to "Come and share our limitless riches! Come and help us bring to light these unimaginable stores of wealth and power!" Of this Adams magnificently approved, and yet (as we shall see) he himself heaped only a "poignant scorn" on the same invitation that was issued by the "speculator" of the Gilded Age, and only anxiety over its acceptance by millions upon millions of poor Europeans then.

How I wish I had already read these earlier words of Adams when I was mounting my own defense of America against the versions of the very same charges that were being lodged in the 1950s by the European philosophers and poets of that era. But it was not until many years later that I came upon Adams's massive *History of the United States of America during the Administrations of Jefferson and Madison,* the book from whose long prologue, "The United States in 1800," the quotations above are taken. When I did, I used them in an essay to refute Adams out of his own mouth. There I pointed out that in attacking the America of the 1880s he sounded exactly like the foreign critics he had derided for their blindness to the poetry of the America of 1800, even though most of the changes that had taken place during those eighty years (including a little item like the abolition of slavery) had, if anything, been for the better.

In accusing Adams of being blind to the political and economic "poetry" of his own time ("The United States themselves," Walt Whitman had once declared, "are essentially the greatest poem"), I would further charge that he had also been dead to its poetry in the more literal sense. He paid no attention to Whitman or Hawthorne or Melville; he rarely read and had no appreciation for the towering novels of his lifelong friend Henry James; and at a time when as great a philosopher as James's older brother William was at the height of his powers, Adams could say, "There is no thought in America."

As it was in the 1800s and then again in the 1880s, so it was in the 1950s. For example, when Stephen Spender and the vast majority of other European "poets and philosophers" carried on against the sins and crimes of capitalist America, they were showing the same blindness that Adams, in his beautifully baroque prose, had exposed in their forebears a century and a half earlier. Staunch lovers of freedom though these contemporary opponents of capitalism believed themselves to be (and actually were in every other realm), they refused or were unable to recognize that the economic system they were denouncing was itself a form of freedom and, on that account alone, to be valued by all who valued freedom. Nor did they show the slightest awareness that this system was achieving a greater degree of more widely shared prosperity, not only in America but wherever it was allowed to operate, than anyone had ever dreamed possible of any set of economic arrangements. Marx had predicted that capitalism would bring about the "progressive immiseration of the poor," but it was already clear to anyone with eyes to see that it was doing the opposite.*

I very much doubt that my own eyes would have been capable of seeing any of this either if not for the arrival at the beginning of my second year at Cambridge of an Australian named Maxwell Newton who had come on a fellowship to "read" for a degree in economics. The existence of this "wild man from the bush," a role he always took special pleasure in playing, first made itself known to me when I was jolted out of a deep sleep one morning by a voice with a thick Australian accent yelling very loudly from the rooms next door to mine that had formerly been occupied by a quiet and sedate Englishman: "For Godsake, Aub, can't you see that I'm whackin' my wire?"

"Aub"—whom I had never before heard anyone address by anything but his full name, Aubrey—was our "gyp," as the college servants at Cambridge were called (at Oxford they were "scouts"), and one of his jobs was to bring us a cup of tea in bed every morning. The usual procedure he followed was to knock gently on our bedroom doors and then, without waiting to be invited in (since the "young gentleman" within would almost always still be asleep), he would enter with his tray. I was unfamiliar with the Australian expression that greeted him and woke me on that particular morning—and so, I daresay, was he—but one did not need to be a scholar of slang to understand that Aubrey had walked in while his newest charge was in the act of pleasuring himself. Yet far from being ashamed or trying to hide, this most peculiar of all the young gentlemen who had ever been placed under Aubrey's care in all the

---

*However, that the shoe was on the other foot—in other words, that Marx's prophecy would ironically turn out to be right as applied to Communism—took much longer to emerge.

decades he had worked as a gyp was more than willing to announce what he had been doing to everyone within earshot of his bellowing voice.

In less than half an hour, Maxwell had barged into my rooms and introduced himself, and from that very first moment we became fast friends. It did not take me long to cotton on to his act, which was deliberately calculated to outrage the "poms"* by riding roughshod over their idea of proper manners, which he regarded, along with almost everything else about the country from which his own people had emigrated, as an antiquated absurdity. It was in line with this strategy that he refused to moderate his Australian accent or to stop using arcane Australian expressions that, as he well knew, were incomprehensible to most Englishmen. He would also take great pleasure in doing things like loudly imitating the sounds of a woman having sexual intercourse as we walked together through the densely packed narrow streets of Cambridge; and the more crowded they were, the greater his joy would be at the sight of these cringing poms.

Little did most of the people who encountered this raw and incorrigibly uncultivated colonial at Cambridge suspect that (among his many other well-concealed accomplishments) he could speak French fluently and with so perfect an accent that once, when he was stopped outside Paris for speeding on his motorcycle and explained in French (throwing in a few esoteric slang terms along the way) that he was an Australian student on vacation who did not know the rules of the French road, the policeman responded with

---

*This, or its variant "pommies," was the derogatory term Australians used for the English. I have never succeeded in tracking down its precise etymology (the *Oxford English Dictionary* says that its origin is obscure), though I always assumed that it was a corruption of the French for potato (*pomme de terre*) and had at some point been transferred from the Irish (who had been called "potato eaters") and applied to all "Brits."

the French equivalent of "Bullshit." How could any foreigner, except perhaps a Belgian, possibly speak French that well? When Maxwell produced his Australian passport, the policeman shook his head in wonder and decided to let this amazing creature go without a ticket.

French, however, was just a sideline to Maxwell, whose real passion was economics. Though most members of the economics faculty at Cambridge were socialists, either of the Marxist or Fabian persuasion, Maxwell was a monetarist, and it was from him that I first heard the name of Milton Friedman. His admiration of the American economy was also as great as his contempt for the system that the Labor government, elected in 1945, had instituted in England. Under socialism, he was convinced, nothing could ever be done right (he positively whooped with vindicated glee at a newsreel in which the first supersonic airplanes, previously advertised to his obstreperous snorts as "a triumph of British scientific and engineering genius," were shown crashing in one test after another). Socialism would also prevent the poms from achieving the prosperity that the relatively free market was generating in the States. Nothing, he assured me, even remotely approaching this prosperity had ever been seen in the history of the world, and he was equally certain that it was only the beginning of even more miraculous levels of wealth ahead.

In spite of his heterodox views, this premature Thatcherite, regarded by almost everyone but me as a disgrace to our college, was so brilliant a student that his suspicious and exasperated socialist examiners were forced to award him a "First," the rough equivalent of a summa cum laude degree in America, except that many fewer such were handed out at Cambridge. Returning to Australia, he would be hired by an ambitious young newspaper publisher there named Rupert Murdoch before falling out with him and then going on to make and lose several large fortunes, while also descending into alcoholism. In the end, coming professionally full circle, he would move to New York to work for Murdoch again.

But even though he had long since stopped drinking, his health had been ruined, and he died in his early sixties, still trumpeting the glories of the American economy, which had more than fulfilled his expectations of it as a young student, and marveling now at the changes in England that Margaret Thatcher's policies had wrought and that he had never expected he would live to see accepted by the intransigently retrograde poms.

Maxwell did not quite succeed in turning me into an enthusiastic proponent of capitalism (a long time would elapse before I was ready to take so drastic a leap). But he did plant the subversive idea in my head that there was nothing wrong with the fact that "the chief business of the American people [was] business," and that, no matter what anyone thought, it was *fortunate* (or rather, "bloody lucky") for the country that there was still as much truth in this notorious observation as there had been when President Calvin Coolidge made it in 1925.

Even so, no honest person looking at America in the 1950s (or for that matter in the 1920s) could have concluded that this was anywhere near the whole truth. The 1920s came to be compared by some to the Gilded Age because of the fortunes being made on the stock market and the corruption of the Harding administration by "big money" (the very phrase John Dos Passos used for the title of the novel covering those years that ended his trilogy, *U.S.A.*). But while "the chief business" of the country may well have been business during that decade, a significant sector of "the American people" was doing other things. Dos Passos himself, along with his friends Ernest Hemingway and F. Scott Fitzgerald, not to mention William Faulkner, were writing their first stories and novels; T. S. Eliot, Ezra Pound, Robert Frost, and e.e. cummings were leading a revolution in poetry; Edmund Wilson, Malcolm Cowley, and Kenneth Burke were producing very important literary criticism. There was excited activity in the other arts as well, ranging from music to architecture, while a rich intellectual life was being conducted by the highly varied likes of John Dewey, Walter Lippmann, and H. L. Mencken.

In the 1950s, too, business was very far from the only activity being pursued by the American people. I would now even contend that a very strong case can be made for describing this much maligned decade as one of the high points of the arts in the history of a country whose main energies—to say it again because it cannot be said too often—had, by the design of its founders, been directed to other areas. I have already noted that Marxists of every sect and sundry other radicals were being driven half crazy by the refusal of America in the 1950s to fulfill their predictions of a postwar depression that would generate a new wave of social protest and political discontent. The revenge they took was to stigmatize this period as "the silent decade." The tag stuck, having come to seem even more appropriate when the wildly contrasting cacophony of the 1960s began piercing the American air.

Yet where cultural activity was concerned, the 1950s were no more "silent" than the 1920s. It was in the 1950s that New York replaced Paris as the center of the art world; it was then that American composers were turning out distinguished music of every kind—classical and popular, jazz and swing, traditional and avant-garde; it was then that American novelists like Saul Bellow, Ralph Ellison, Norman Mailer, and Philip Roth began coming into their own; it was then that poets like Robert Lowell, John Berryman, Marianne Moore, Wallace Stevens, Theodore Roethke, and others too numerous to mention were doing some of their best work; it was then that so many formidable literary critics were around that one of them (Randall Jarrell, who was also a poet) complained that we were living in "The Age of Criticism." There were even social critics like C. Wright Mills, whose work was an early warning sign of the radicalism to come in the 1960s.

At the time, in defending America, I did not yet have all these names at my command. But I was caught up in a new mood that had begun developing in earnest among writers and intellectuals just as I was leaving for England, and whenever I made an effort to describe what was going on back home, I would invariably fish up a line from a poem by John Donne which went, "O my America, my Newfoundland!" Donne (writing long before his transformation into the Dean of St. Paul's Cathedral) had of course been speaking metaphorically in the special witty fashion of the Metaphysical poets about the body of a woman he was just setting out to explore. But even if this was how the image was intended in the seventeenth century, at the midpoint of the twentieth it made perfect sense when read literally as an expression of the attitude that had overtaken many American intellectuals. America truly was a land being newly found or discovered; and the explorers in this instance were formerly "alienated" writers and intellectuals. A large number of them even participated in a symposium published under the startling rubric "Our Country and Our Culture" published in 1952 in *Partisan Review*, which had once prided itself on, precisely, its alienation from American society.

I have referred to this symposium several times in my past writings because it has always seemed to me one of the most telling indications of the profound change in the attitudes toward America that took place in the upper reaches of the literary culture in the early part of the 1950s. A year later, in 1953, the same change achieved expression through the medium of fiction in Saul Bellow's novel *The Adventures of Augie March*. "I am an American, Chicago-born," it began in a tone of identification with this country that anyone—anyone, that is, with ears to hear and a sense of the intellectual and literary tradition from which Bellow had emerged—immediately recognized as defiant; and it ended with the narrator comparing his fate to that of Columbus, who had been brought home in chains from the land he had been the first to discover, which, declared Augie in the last sentence of the novel, "didn't prove there was no America."

· · ·

To be sure, not everyone experienced this "American high" or joined in the "American celebration," as the new mood would respectively be characterized by the historian William L. O'Neill and the socialist literary critic Irving Howe. In addition to Howe, among the dissenters was Bellow's great friend, Delmore Schwartz. Though he would write a rave review of *The Adventures of Augie March* in *Partisan Review* itself, ranking it with no less great a novel than *Adventures of Huckleberry Finn*, Schwartz in his contribution just a year earlier to the *PR* symposium had denounced the abandonment it constituted of the traditions of alienation and of "critical nonconformism." Yet by 1958, in another key passage I have always loved to quote because it so saliently epitomized the new spirit among the literary intellectuals, even Schwartz fell into step:

> Clearly when the future of civilization is no longer assured, a criticism of American life in terms of a contrast between avowed ideals and present actuality cannot be a primary preoccupation and source of inspiration. For America, not Europe, is now the sanctuary of culture; civilization's very existence depends upon America, upon the actuality of American life, and not the ideals of the American Dream. To criticize the actuality upon which all hope depends thus becomes a criticism of hope itself.

By the time Schwartz wrote these words, I was long gone from Cambridge and out of the army too, working as a junior editor on the staff of *Commentary*. But throughout the five (or more nearly six) years I was away, I had kept up avidly as a reader with the "American celebration," and then began joining in on it as a young literary and social critic. Much of the ammunition I used in upholding America against the contemptuous, hostile, and largely ignorant European views of it came not only from the books I have already mentioned but also from articles in *Partisan Review*. However, *Commentary*, founded in 1945 and thus about ten years younger than *Partisan Review*, was an even richer source. Under its first editor, Elliot E. Cohen, *Commentary* was wholehearted in its embrace of America and much more consistent in its passion to show just how beautiful "America the Beautiful" was. *Partisan Review*, on the other hand, was always so uncomfortable about its new pro-American stance that it felt obliged to open its own pages to denunciations such as, most notoriously, "This Age of Conformity" by Irving Howe.

In this essay, published in 1954, Howe accused his fellow intellectuals of betraying their calling, just as Julien Benda had even more explosively done before him in 1927 in his book, *La Trahison des Clercs* ("The Treason of the Intellectuals"). There Benda had attacked an analogous embrace of French nationalism as a form of treason to the internationalist perspective which he believed it was the duty of intellectuals to adopt and foster. For tactical reasons having to do with the nonsectarian appeal he was aiming at, Howe never said in so many words that to him the perspective demanding loyalty from the intellectuals was not internationalism in general but socialism in particular. Unlike his fellow former Trotskyist Dwight Macdonald, who with his usual devil-may-care bluntness had come right out and denounced all those who, their judgment allegedly distorted by the fevers of World War Two, had been so philistine and so retrograde as to deny "the overmastering reality of our age: the decomposition of the bourgeois synthesis in all fields,"* Howe adopted a softer approach. He blandly presented as an axiom precisely the assumption that was now being questioned—"that the whole idea of the intellectual vocation" was "of a life dedicated to values that cannot possibly be realized by a commercial civilization."

In explaining why this idea was gradually losing its "allure" and making the intellectuals "tame," Howe could not altogether free

---

*There is a fuller discussion of Macdonald's position in Part Three.

himself of the socialist habit of interpreting any defection from what was so obviously the true faith as a form of "selling out" to the capitalist enemy for money or power. But on this issue too he prudently refrained from putting all his cards on the table, being intelligent enough to understand that to make this vulgar charge entirely explicit would weaken his case.* Again he went for a milder version of the traditional charge: "Some intellectuals, to be sure, have 'sold out'. . . . But far more prevalent and far more insidious is that slow attrition which destroys one's ability to stand firm and alone."

When "This Age of Conformity" appeared, I was stationed at Fort Devens in Massachusetts where I was getting advanced training before being sent overseas (to, as it would turn out, Germany rather than Korea). Never having met Howe, but knowing that he was on the faculty of Brandeis, which was located only a short distance away, I decided to call him up and ask if I could come see him on my next weekend pass. He recognized my name from the reviews I had already published in both *Partisan Review* and *Commentary* and readily agreed to a visit.

It did not go well. As a much younger member of the "Family" of New York intellectuals than he was (twenty-four to his thirty-four), and still given to a certain deference to my elders, I could not quite summon the nerve to tell him that "This Age of Conformity" had struck me as wrongheaded and regressive in its stubborn resistance to a development that I felt was necessary to the health of our culture. But the debate that telling him this was sure to have triggered between us would at least have been better than what happened when I tried to avoid engaging him head-on. This I did by saying that being in the army was beginning to make the issues

---

*Another problem was that he himself, being a book reviewer for Henry Luce's *Time*, was vulnerable to the same charge, as Robert Warshow did not fail to point out in a devastating rebuttal. Warshow, my editor and mentor at *Commentary*, would die of a heart attack at the age of thirty-seven when I was still in the army.

he had raised seem much less important than I had thought they were before. "Well," he responded, no doubt to some extent—but only to some extent—out of wounded author's vanity, "if that's so, maybe you should consider going into another line of work." I can still practically feel the intense red heat—half of embarrassment and half of anger—that this remark brought to my face. The embarrassment was all mine, and even the anger was as much directed at myself for having been so foolish as at him for having been so cruel.

Yet the funny thing was that I was telling the truth: not the whole truth and nothing but the truth, but enough of it so that I would not have made such a fool of myself if I had not been afraid that I might have made an even greater fool of myself if I had gone on to explain what I meant. Which was this: Howe's essay had primarily distressed me because it rained on my parade. To me it had been a wonder, and a personal delight, to see the writers and intellectuals I most admired, and whose company I aspired to join, endorsing the patriotism that had been bred into my bones from childhood and that came so much more naturally to me than the "alienation" I would once have been expected to feel if I were to be accepted as one of them. It was this that I lacked the courage to say to Howe, not yet having figured out how to put it in terms that would have sounded sophisticated enough for him to take seriously even while entirely disagreeing with me.

What I did work up the courage to say, however, was less than fully truthful only because I *did* try to put it in terms that I thought he would consider intellectually respectable. Surely this brilliant man, having himself been in the army in World War Two, would understand and even sympathize with a younger intellectual whose experience of being a soldier was giving him a different perspective on the relative significance in life of the ideological issues that were central to an essay like "This Age of Conformity." But as it happens, Irving Howe—as I would learn in the future when I got to know him well—was the last man in the world to whom such an idea would appeal. Least of all at a moment when he regarded himself as a lonely upholder of the true faith against the mass apostasies occurring all around him.

In this new perspective of mine that was being shaped by the army, America was turning from the abstraction it had been to me as a kid in Brooklyn, and then the ideological issue it had become in my arguments at Cambridge and elsewhere in Europe, into a concrete reality. I hated the army at first and basic training at Fort Dix in New Jersey during a very cold winter was almost more than I could bear. But I did bear it, and even became, to my own great surprise and even greater gratification, a pretty good soldier. And what surprised me as well was how much I liked my barracks mates wherever I went during my two years in the army. Never before, not even at Columbia, had I met so many different American types, and the easy relations I formed with them made me realize all over again that this was the only country in which I could feel fully at home.

I came to know all these types well, and I got a different kick out of every one of them. There were the midwesterners, one of whom would invariably be the first person to greet you with a cheery "Hi, there" whenever you were transferred to a new company, but to whom you never got any closer than that no matter how long you lived and worked together.* There were the southerners whose touchy sense of honor was familiar to me from the borrowed form it took among the transplanted Negroes with whom I had grown up in Brooklyn, and who were always ready to spring to a buddy's defense with a broken beer bottle whenever a fight broke out in a bar. Some of my closest friends in the army

---

*The only major exception I would ever encounter was the midwesterner I would marry a year after being discharged and to whom I am still married after more than forty years.

were "rednecks" of this kind, one of whom once explained to me that I was popular among them because I "talked so good."

Then there were the rebels against army discipline, working-class kids from places like Pittsburgh and Detroit, who always seemed to have great senses of humor that I thought were peculiarly and uniquely American. In Kassel, Germany, one of these guys had posted a notice written in crayon on cardboard that was the first thing I saw upon entering the barracks to which I had just been assigned. Addressed in a delicious mélange of English and German to soldiers returning drunk from a pass and warning them against throwing up on the premises, it read, NIX BARFEN ZIE IN DER HALL.

At every opportunity, the author of this injunction, who shortly became another great friend of mine, went "*schatzi* hunting," as in his inimitable style he described looking for German girls to pick up, which he always found easier to do than getting them into bed with his plaintive pleas of "Wanten zie schlaffen mit me?" Sometimes he would persuade me to accompany him on these expeditions on the theory that, since I actually could speak a little German, my propositions would work better. Alas for both of us, the theory never proved out. On one occasion the situation had looked promising, but the two German girls we met, whose fathers had for all I knew been in the SS, changed their minds at the last minute. Their excuse was that, having just seen Marlon Brando brutally beaten in the movie *On the Waterfront*, they were afraid to get mixed up with such violent men as Americans evidently were.

I had not yet been to Germany when I visited Irving Howe, but I had experienced enough in the year I had already spent in uniform for my sense of what America, and Americans, were like in the flesh to feel that there was something seriously wrong with his ideologically driven hostility to the "actuality of American life." Like many socialists, he did not, I think, have much feel or affection for the individuals who made up the working classes and the poor out of whose ranks he had risen and of which he saw himself as a spokesman and a champion. It was in the mass, and as the masses, that he loved them, if indeed he loved them at all instead of just offering them a "compassion" that consisted less of personal sympathy than of a concept of social organization that was supposedly in their best interest.

I too had moved up out of those same ranks, and when I was pushed back down into them as an enlisted man in the army after living the life of a "young English gentleman," I thought I might have trouble finding my way around. But nothing of the sort happened. Nor, even after being educated at two of the best universities in the world, and facing a future that would inevitably elevate me once again to a higher social and economic status than most of my army buddies were likely to reach, did I ever feel in the least bit superior to them. Just the opposite: I would come out of the army with a new respect for the ordinary guys among whom I had lived for two years, and a deeper and greater love of the country we all shared and of which they were the true backbone. "The good sense of the American people" might become a tiresome cliché in the mouths of cheap politicians, but after serving in the army, I would always think of it as one of the most "self-evident" of the truths on which the republic had been founded.

PART

"Look! We Have Come Through!"

Jacques Barzun, a professor of history at Columbia with whom I took a course or two, was a native of France who had come to America when very young ("in ridiculous short pants and ignorant of baseball") and had mastered English to the point where he could not only write it elegantly but could also give instruction in proper English usage and style. Although he became a very close friend of his colleague in the English department, Lionel Trilling, together with whom he often taught a special seminar, he had only a distant and tenuous connection with the "Family" of New York intellectuals centered around *Partisan Review* and *Commentary*, of which Trilling himself was a leading member.

Never mind that he was by a large measure more learned than most of them and as a cultural historian had even broader interests. For example, along with a number of other authoritative books about the nineteenth century like *Romanticism and the Modern Ego*, he was capable of turning out the definitive biography in two fat volumes of Hector Berlioz, a then (1949) unfashionable composer to whose work I would guess most of the New York intellectuals had never paid any attention or of which some of them may well never even have heard, their indifference to music being for some reason as great as their passion for literature and painting. (Perhaps in this respect I was not as unique as I thought; perhaps they too, like me, had been denied music lessons as children.*)

---

*So far as I can recall, the only composer who frequented that circle was Israel Citkowitz. He had been considered very promising in his youth, but had then

In spite of all this, and even though *Partisan Review* published a few pieces by Barzun (under pressure, I suspect, from Trilling, who was a member of its advisory board), the *PR* inner circle still grumbled about his work, regarding it as a species of popularization that belonged more naturally to the "middlebrow" world of magazines like *Harper's* and the *Atlantic*. Without knowing for sure, I would guess that (making an exception only for Trilling) Barzun's attitude toward them was no more admiring than theirs toward him. Why else would he quote with such relish an anonymous "parody epitaph that was once applied to the half-fascist, half-Communist suffering from 'alienation' "?:

> I worshiped none, for fear of being an ass;
> Nietzsche I liked, but more than Nietzsche Sartre;
> I played both sides against the middle class:
> It shrinks, and I am heading for Montmartre.

Be that as it may, Barzun was even more fully caught up in "the American celebration" than the intellectuals Irving Howe took out against in "This Age of Conformity." In fact, in 1954, just months after Howe's essay appeared in *Partisan Review*, Barzun published a book entitled *God's Country and Mine*, which was at least as guilty of the sins that Howe excoriated the members of his own intellec-

---

been afflicted by a block, and had written nothing for a long time. Once I told him my sad story, adding that the only piece I could play was the upper part of "Heart and Soul" on the piano with one finger. So amused, and touched, was he that he promised to compose a concerto around that theme and to enlist me as the soloist. He actually tried doing this, but alas, his block got the better of him, and we both remained musically where we started. Being handsome, charming, and intelligent, however, he went on to snare an heiress, Lady Caroline Freud (of the Guinness Stout family), a writer who had formerly been married to the painter Lucien Freud, and who would later leave "Lord Citkowitz," as he was cruelly called in the Family, for the poet Robert Lowell.

tual circle for committing. The difference was that Barzun, never having been any kind of Marxist or socialist, could not be accused of apostasy or "selling out." In celebrating America, he was building a case against the traditional European condescension or outright hostility toward his adopted country—the kind of attitude whose *locus classicus* was in the sneer attributed to Georges Clemencau which I quoted earlier. "Can it be true," Barzun asked,

> that Americanization is tantamount to barbarization? Or is it possible that modern civilization is something new, incommensurable with the old, just like the character of the American adventure itself? One may want to give a just answer and yet feel that, whatever the answer, the time has come when America must no longer take scoldings with humility.

Barzun was thus closer to his fellow historian across the sea, D. W. Brogan, than he was to the New York intellectuals who had newly become aware of some of the virtues of a country they had formerly despised in every respect and from which they had indeed felt alienated.

But Barzun did have at least have one thing in common with the New York intellectuals. Like them, he experienced a certain uneasiness over the possibility that he might be going too far in the other direction. In his case, going too far did not mean giving up the role of "critical nonconformism" that, as Delmore Schwartz sternly reminded them, the New York intellectuals had regarded as their proper duty. It meant, rather, paying insufficient deference to the European contempt for America as a crass and uncivilized country, lacking in high culture and refined manners alike, and dedicated exclusively to the pursuit of material goods. Out of this uneasiness came the subtitle Barzun gave to *God's Country and Mine:* "A Declaration of Love Spiced with a Few Harsh Words." It was a subtitle that foreshadowed a compulsion evident throughout the book to acknowledge the force of the standard European criticisms of America (including a number for which Barzun himself clearly had little or no use) before going on to answer them, often in what struck me as excessively defensive terms.

Reading Barzun's book when it was first published, I thought this subtitle and the defensiveness it prefigured marred an otherwise admirably courageous project. My own feeling was that enough harsh words had already been, and were still being, spoken about America and that no additional ones were needed.* It even seemed to me that the need Barzun felt to include even a few such words within an overall "declaration of love" amounted to a reverse "loyalty oath," which was no less deplorable than the one government employees and others were being forced to sign in order to prove that they were not involved in any conspiracy to overthrow the government of the United States.

Why, I asked myself, was it any different or any better when intellectuals were coerced into demonstrating loyalty to the traditional pieties of their own community on pain not so much of losing their jobs as of losing their good names and even being branded as guilty of their own brand of treason (that is, Benda's "*la trahison des clercs*")? Where Barzun was concerned, those pieties were rooted more firmly in European than American soil. But since the American ethos of alienation of which he made fun

---

*Another of Barzun's fellow historians—this one in America—disagreed. In writing about the book for *Partisan Review*, Arthur Schlesinger, Jr. (who had never been a Marxist or ever suffered from a feeling of alienation) commended Barzun for his love of America, but criticized him for erring "in the direction of rapture." Barzun, he said, was "more vivid and convincing in attack than in affirmation." Of course, for Schlesinger, a fiercely partisan Democrat, America could not be truly great when the White House was occupied by a Republican like Dwight Eisenhower. This was clear even then, but Schlesinger made it almost embarrassingly explicit about ten years later in his book about the Kennedy administration, where he wrote that after JFK had succeeded Eisenhower as President, "Intelligence *at last* was being applied to public affairs. . . ." The italics are mine.

through the anonymous parody he quoted had (as he himself recognized) at least partly been imported from the anti-bourgeois traditions of European aristocrats, artists, and intellectuals, and focused on many of the same issues, this could seem a distinction without a difference.

Considering how I would shortly react to Barzun's defensiveness, one might have thought that in 1953, I would greet Saul Bellow's novel *The Adventures of Augie March* with enormous enthusiasm as the first unapologetic fictional fruit of the "American celebration." And so I would have done had the fruit been ripe. But Bellow—a man of immense intelligence who had sensed which way the wind was about to blow almost before anyone else could detect even the stirring of a breeze—had immediately rushed out to fill his choking lungs with this oncoming breath of fresh air. Too impatient to wait for the new wind to shake the fruit out of the tree and onto the ground, he climbed up and yanked it off himself when it was still sour to the taste and hard to digest.

To translate this perhaps overly complicated metaphor into the terms of literary criticism, I thought that Bellow's affirmation of America in *Augie March* sounded forced and unconvincing and therefore made for a novel that was unsuccessful from a literary point of view. The reason it failed, in my judgment, was that, unaware (or, more likely, unwilling to admit to himself) that he had not yet quite been liberated from the old attitudes toward America to which the novel was issuing a multifaceted challenge, he had to strain too hard to express the new ones.

This many-sided challenge manifested itself, first of all, in an experimental prose style. It was a style that married (as Mark Twain's had done in *Adventures of Huckleberry Finn*, the book from which, according to Ernest Hemingway, "all modern American literature comes" and which, as Delmore Schwartz correctly perceived, had served as Bellow's inspiration and model here) the cultivated with the colloquial. But Bellow also laced this mixture (as, obviously, Mark Twain, had not done) with rhythms and idioms drawn from Yiddish.*

Unlike the experiments with language of the modernist tradition on which Bellow had been raised, however, his was genuinely original in expressing not an attempt to ignore the philistines and wall them off, but the very opposite: it was expressing a sense of joyous connection with the common grain of American life as he himself, a Jew from Chicago, knew it at first hand. In 1916, James Joyce, speaking through his protagonist Stephen Dedalus in his first novel, *A Portrait of the Artist as a Young Man*, gave voice to a similar sentiment in a proclamation that would become one of the great battle cries of the entire modernist movement: "Welcome, O life! I go to encounter for the millionth time the reality of experience and to forge in the smithy of my soul the uncreated conscience of my race." But in pursuing this intention, what Joyce went on to produce was *Ulysses* and then *Finnegans Wake*, the first of which was scarcely comprehensible to his "race" and the second entirely impenetrable. In this respect, Bellow was much closer to Mark Twain in reaching out to the audience than he was to James Joyce who, upon being asked how he expected anyone to understand *Finnegans Wake*, replied in all seriousness: "The demand that I make of my reader is that he should devote his whole life to reading my works."

As with the prose, so with the hero. In certain aspects, Augie March was a familiar figure, an image of modern man living in a hopelessly fluid society, forced to forge an identity because he had inherited none, and unable to find a settled place for himself. He

---

*Bellow's Yiddish was much better than mine. When he was still an adolescent, he and his equally precocious pal Isaac Rosenfeld collaborated on a brilliant parody in Yiddish of T. S. Eliot's "The Love Song of J. Alfred Prufrock." Never in a million years could I have done such a thing.

was, in short, yet another embodiment of alienation. But he did not respond to this condition as did the characters in Bellow's first two novels (*Dangling Man* and *The Victim*), or most other products of what the transplanted British poet W. H. Auden had earlier called "The Age of Anxiety." On the contrary: he was "larky and boisterous," and his rootless condition made life not a torment but endlessly adventurous and bursting with surprise. Even his uncertainty about his own identity was represented as a positive advantage, not leading to the usual narcissistic self-involvement but breeding a readiness to explore the world, a generous openness to experience.

In short, Bellow imbued Augie March with a quality that was the rarest of any to be found in the heroes of the modern novel: he made him an optimist. Not a blind or naïve optimist like Voltaire's Candide, but one who understood that there were powerful arguments against his position and that it was a faith which, like any other, had to struggle to maintain itself in the teeth of the opposing evidence. "You want to accept," one of his friends tells him. "But how do you know what you're accepting? . . . You should accept the data of experience." To which Augie replies: "It can never be right to offer to die, and if that's what the data of experience tell you, then you must get along without them."

In addition to the prose style Bellow created for this novel, then, he invented a hero who looked around him and saw neither bleakness nor soullessness nor the blandness of "conformity" but rather richness and glory. There were treasures all sitting there waiting to be dug up by anyone with the guts and the imagination to go prospecting for them, and these, Bellow was tacitly asserting, included a cast of characters no less fabulous than the ones Charles Dickens had unearthed in Victorian England. Following Augie in his "adventures," we no longer came upon the puny creatures of Bellow's earlier novels who were forever taking their own pulses and dragging themselves onerously from one day to the next. Now we were introduced on practically every page to huge figures whom Augie aggressively and defiantly compared to Caesar, Machiavelli, Ulysses, and Croesus ("I'm not kidding," he insisted, "when I enter Einhorn in this eminent list").

Having wrought such a prose style and created such a hero, Bellow thought (and so did many of the New York intellectuals to whose company he belonged, Chicagoan though he was) that he had finally broken through. He, along with most of them, had been looking for a route out of the impasse at which, they rightly believed, the ethos of alienation had arrived, and with *The Adventures of Augie March* he felt confident that he had hit upon it. It was a route that led to the chance of participating fully in the American life of the time without loss of individuality or integrity, and that simultaneously pointed toward a fusion of mind and experience, sophistication and vitality, intelligence and power.

The problem was that this unquestionably desirable, and even noble, project failed as literature because it was largely willed. By this I mean that it was not the natural, organic outgrowth of a state of being already achieved but rather the product of an effort on Bellow's part to act as though he had already achieved it. Admittedly, at isolated moments, the prose style worked just as Bellow wanted it to do, achieving exactly the extraordinary effects he was after:

> [Mama] occupied a place, I suppose, among women conquered by a superior force of love, like those women whom Zeus got the better of in animal form and who next had to take cover from his furious wife. Not that I can see my big, gentle, dilapidated, scrubbing, and lugging mother as a fugitive of immense beauty from such classy wrath. . . .

But the rightness, the poise, and the easy mastery of this passage were not typical of *Augie* as a whole. More often, Bellow seemed to be twisting and torturing the language in an almost hysterical battle to wring all the juices out of it:

The rest of us had to go to the dispensary—which was like the dream of a multitude of dentists' chairs, hundreds of them in a space as enormous as an armory, and green bowls with designs of glass, grapes, grills lifted zigzag as insects' legs, and gas flames on the porcelain swivel trays—a thundery gloom in Harrison Street of limestone county buildings and cumbersome red streetcars with metal grillwork on their windows and monarchical iron whiskers of cowcatchers front and rear. They lumbered and clanged, and their brake tanks panted in the slushy brown of a winter afternoon or the bare stone brown of a summer's, salted with ash, smoke, and prairie dust, with long stops at the clinics to let off clumpers, cripples, hunchbacks, brace-legs, crutch-wielders, tooth and eye sufferers, and all the rest.

The frantic and feverish pitch here betrayed the basic uncertainty that I have been pointing to in *Augie March:* it told us that there was simply not enough real conviction behind the attitudes out of which the novel was written.

So too with the character of Augie himself. He was portrayed as someone whose very existence constituted a refutation of "the data of experience" forming the foundation of the ethos against which Bellow was rebelling. But to be convincing, such a refutation would have needed a series of confrontations between Augie and those "data" leading to a correlative series of struggles that would strengthen and deepen his "own way of going at things." Yet nothing like this happens to Augie, who is curiously untouched by his adventures, who never changes or develops, who goes through everything and undergoes nothing.

If, then, Bellow was refusing to sign a "loyalty oath" to the old orthodoxies of the intellectual tradition out of which he had emerged; and if (all honor to him for this) he was not even looking nervously over his (left) shoulder as he wrote and trying to protect himself with propitiatory gestures to the pieties of the past, this stubborn ethos nevertheless remained powerful enough to hold him back from a full literary or aesthetic realization of the breakthrough to which (and all honor to him for this as well) he aspired.

I angered a great many people—Bellow himself most of all—by making these points in no uncertain terms in the review I wrote for *Commentary* while I was a "dangling man" myself, waiting to be drafted into the army. But there were others who applauded, including even Bellow's lifelong friend Isaac Rosenfeld. To the extent that so exuberantly raucous and outspoken a character was capable of doing so, he whispered his agreement into my ear (while—no doubt for fear of being cut off if he were frank with so touchy a writer as he knew his old buddy to be—telling Bellow himself in private how much he admired the novel). The irrepressible Dwight Macdonald, on the other hand, shouted his approval from the rooftops, and so did Philip Rahv, the co-editor of *Partisan Review*.

But there was a taint in the support I got from Rosenfeld, Macdonald, Rahv, and others like them. I understood (even, or perhaps especially, at an age when I was burning with ambition myself) that Rosenfeld could hardly help experiencing more than a touch of envy at the wholly unexpected and even incredible sight (for that period) of a "highbrow" novel like *Augie March* on the *New York Times* best-seller list when he was still laboring in the obscure cultural thickets out of which Bellow, without so much as a suspicion of having compromised his literary standards, had now hacked himself into the sun by day and the spotlight by night. Yet even leaving aside such considerations, I took less satisfaction than I might have done from the approval I received for attacking *Augie March* because in my heart I knew that it came from the opposite direction in which I, trailing after Bellow himself, had been steadily moving.

For me, the aesthetic failures of *Augie March* were a disappointment. Although I was a great believer in the autonomy of art, I was not the kind of full-fledged aesthete for whom its purpose, in the notorious phrase of the Victorian English critic Walter Pater, was "to discern a shade on the hills a little lovelier than the rest." For I also thought that the serious literature of a country, *properly read*, carried significant clues to the true state of affairs in the society of which it was inevitably, *though not solely*, a reflection. I have put those words in italics to emphasize the difference between this approach to literature and the one that guided literary critics on the opposite extreme from Pater—critics of the Left to whom art was a "weapon," and who praised or damned novels and poems and plays entirely for the political or ideological positions they took, and not for how well or badly the writer's intentions—whatever they might be—were realized. As to those intentions, my position was derived from Henry James's dictum that the novelist must be permitted his *"donné"*—he was not to be judged for what he chose to write about, but only for how well he wrote about it (which did not preclude moral judgment afterward).

With none of this would Isaac Rosenfeld or Dwight Macdonald or Philip Rahv (or, for that matter, Irving Howe) have found anything wrong: certainly not in theory. But what disappointed me about *Augie March* was precisely what pleased them. Indeed, I was scarcely exaggerating when I later remarked that the validity of a whole new phase of American culture had at that time been felt to be riding on whether or not *Augie March* was really a great novel. Like me, Rosenfeld, Macdonald, and the rest took the novel's failures to mean that the newly positive feeling toward America which had just begun to show itself within the intellectual community was still half-baked and shot through with uncertainty. In my eyes (as I had vainly and foolishly tried explaining to Irving Howe) this was a deplorable sign of the powerful hold retained by archaic ideas on writers who were being inhibited in their efforts to do something fresh and new such as Bellow had attempted. But most of my supporters among the critics of *Augie March* were gratified

by this evidence of the continuing grip of the traditionally negative perspective on this country and its culture. For it was a perspective which they still regarded as largely, or even entirely, valid.

This was why even some who had been willing to accept the
pronoun "our" in the title of the *Partisan Review* symposium on
"Our Country and Our Culture" had done so only grudgingly and
only with enough "harsh words" thrown in to keep them from going too far in the direction of outright approval or, worse, a "declaration of love." Rosenfeld (though having long since abandoned
his youthful commitment to Trotskyism) still regarded himself as
an alienated radical: in a swipe at the fashionable talk of those days
about the "the need for roots," Rosenfeld quipped that "the ideal
society . . . cannot afford to include many deeply rooted intellectuals." Macdonald (for all the dizzying zigs and zags that had already
carried him from Trotskyism to pacifism to anarchism—and he
was not through zigging and zagging yet) still bore within him the
person he was in 1941, when he had written in vitriolic terms
about the critic Van Wyck Brooks and the poet Archibald
MacLeish (then the Librarian of Congress) for having become so
"reactionary" as to question "the overmastering reality of our age:
the decomposition of the bourgeois synthesis in all fields."* And it

---

*Macdonald had even associated MacLeish and Brooks both with the Nazis
and the Stalinists. MacLeish's crime was a notorious speech entitled "The Irre-
sponsibles" he had delivered as Librarian of Congress in the early days of World
War Two (before the United States had entered it). There MacLeish accused the
disillusioned novels about World War One by writers like Ernest Hemingway
and John Dos Passos—as well as certain of his own works—of having "done more
to disarm democracy in the face of fascism than any other single influence" by
fostering cynicism among the young generation. Subsequently Brooks also made
a speech in which he had the effrontery to downgrade as "secondary" the contemporary literary avant-garde for being obscure and negative and out of touch with
"the collective life of the people." These two speeches, railed Macdonald, embodied the Nazi concept of *Kulturbolshewismus* (or "cultural Bolshevism") combined with "the specific values of Stalinism." In characterizing the somewhat

was Rahv himself who, as the co-editor of *Partisan Review*, must have at least signed off on the symposium's title, and yet who immediately turned around and encouraged Irving Howe to write "This Age of Conformity" in order to deflect his own magazine from the path on which it had set a hesitant foot.

All this was a sign of things to come. Rosenfeld, who died of a heart attack in 1956 at the age of thirty-eight, did not live long enough to be affected by the upheavals of the 1960s, but it is hard to imagine that he would have responded to them much differently from Macdonald and Rahv. Both of these latter had, as passionate anti-Stalinists (which Rosenfeld was too) strongly supported the American side in the cold war, but they completely flip-flopped in the 1960s. Macdonald eventually became so wild an opponent of the American intervention in Vietnam that, when he was invited by Lyndon Johnson as part of a group of intellectuals to a White House ceremony honoring the arts, he spent his entire time there circulating a petition denouncing his host. Moreover, so enthusiastic an admirer of the antiwar radicals on the campuses did he become that, when a gang of them seized and occupied the office of the president of Columbia University in 1968, he could not wait to express his solidarity by getting himself hoisted up in a basket to

---

dissimilar positions of MacLeish and Brooks as an "ominous sign of the drift toward totalitarianism" that he saw taking place in America, Macdonald actually claimed to be doing so "Not in the spirit of abuse but as a sober historical description." [!] To be clear about my own position, I should add that I bring all this up not to defend MacLeish and Brooks. Their ideas were certainly open to serious challenge (and indeed were attacked by other critics like Edmund Wilson and Lionel Trilling, who did not, however, smear them as Nazi and/or Stalinist). My purpose, rather, is to show how powerfully entrenched among many American intellectuals were the attitudes from which Bellow was trying to free himself, and the abuse that might lie in store for any writer who dared to say a good word for "bourgeois values" (a term Macdonald himself used in the *Partisan Review* essay —reprinted in his book *Memoirs of a Revolutionist*—from which I have been quoting).

join them. (So, by the way, during a visit from London to New York, did Stephen Spender, possibly to "prove" his contention that he had been duped by the CIA into becoming co-editor of *Encounter.*)

Rahv went even further. In 1952, he had written an admiring, if not uncritical, piece about Whittaker Chambers's *Witness* (put off, as a militant atheist, by the emphasis on religion in Chambers's worldview, he still acknowledged the literary distinction of the book and its great value as a historical document). Yet by the end of the 1960s he had become what another critic, Frederick Crews, not without reason, derided as a "born-again Leninist." There was, however, a complication here. Admiring though he was of the New Left of the 1960s, which he praised as the most significant radical movement to have appeared in America since the 1930s, Rahv had no use for its cultural manifestations. In this he differed so strongly with his co-editor William Phillips that he resigned from *Partisan Review* to found a new magazine. Its name was *Modern Occasions*, and its purpose was to back the politics of the New Left and attack its liberal opponents (Lionel Trilling, for example), while at the same time excoriating its allies in the counterculture such as Susan Sontag (for whose work, much of which was being published in *Partisan Review*, Rahv had a special distaste). The project was inherently unstable, and *Modern Occasions* lasted only a very short time.

But then there was Bellow. Like Augie March, his creator "went at things [his] own way, free-style" in the 1960s. On the one hand, Bellow kept his distance from almost every camp (and there were many more than just two) formed to fight the battles of the period; and his commitment to the wall of separation between art and politics was as great as that of the ACLU to the separation between church and state. On the other hand, no close reader of the novels that came after *Augie March*—especially what may be the best of them, *Mr. Sammler's Planet* (1970)—could miss his contempt for the radicalism of the 1960s, especially on its cultural side, and his anger over the sorry pass to which it had helped bring the country.

I followed a different course, though I too went at things in my own way. It was not a way that could be characterized as "free-style," but it did have its peculiar wrinkles and contours that never quite corresponded to anyone else's. I was never even entirely at one with the friends and colleagues and collaborators I acquired when I became the editor-in-chief of *Commentary* in 1960 and transformed it (for reasons that will become clear in a moment) into an exponent of a then nascent new radicalism. Nor did I quite see eye to eye with the friends and colleagues and collaborators who replaced them when, ten years later, after a bout of disillusioning experiences, I turned into a fierce critic of what the new radicalism had by that point become.

All love affairs run into rocky patches, and this complicated set of developments in my thinking might be seen as the one in which mine with America got stuck for a number of years until a reconciliation carried it to greater heights of passion and fidelity than it had ever reached before. In a way, it was less like a love affair than a marriage in crisis that never reached the extreme of divorce and that, having weathered the storm, emerged in so strengthened a condition that the partners could truly now vow that only death would do them part.

My affair with America entered its rocky patch in the late 1950s, when I began feeling and saying that the social and political conditions around me were barricading the road to a richer and more exciting life. But it was when I took over *Commentary* in 1960 after the death of Elliot E. Cohen that things really got rough.

Under Cohen, who had created *Commentary* in 1945, the magazine had been having a love affair of its own with America. So much so that it was altogether appropriate for Mary McCarthy's "America the Beautiful" to have appeared in its pages rather than in *Partisan Review*, which was her regular venue. For as

I have already indicated, it was Cohen, and not William Phillips or Philip Rahv or any other member of the New York intellectual Family, who became the true pioneer in the exploration and rediscovery of America during the decade or so immediately following World War Two.

Like Phillips and Rahv, Cohen had briefly been a Communist in the early 1930s and then, in breaking, had become a staunch and passionate anti-Communist. But to a far greater extent than they, or many other Jews who had followed the same course,* he grew more and more persuaded that the true home of the Jewish people was America. To revert once more to the odious terms that were standard in the discussion of this entire issue, the "solution" to the "Jewish problem" did not in his view lie in the establishment of a sovereign Jewish state in Palestine such as the Zionists dreamed of, and against which he stood firm until the state was actually founded. Nor, on the other side, did the "solution" lie in a gradual disappearance through assimilation. What Cohen envisaged was the building up of a Jewish community in America that was proud of and knowledgeable about its heritage and could strive to preserve it without sacrificing one whit of its wholly legitimate, commendable, and— this was the key point—realistic or viable ambition to enter fully into the life of the surrounding American society.

In the "Golden Age" of medieval Spain before the expulsion of the Jews in 1492, Cohen saw a forerunner (all differences acknowledged) of his vision of America. I never asked him whether he attached any mystical significance, as I could not (and cannot) stop myself from doing, to the coincidence that in the very same year the Jews were expelled from Spain, Columbus (himself suspected

---

*It is still not well understood that, while a majority of the members of the American Communist party was probably of Jewish origin, only a small minority of the American Jewish community *as a whole* belonged to or was sympathetic to the Communist party. Like my father, most American Jews were Roosevelt-worshiping liberals.

by some scholars as having been of Jewish origin) should have discovered America: a Golden Age of diaspora Jewish culture being replaced by what the Yiddish-speaking immigrants who came here between the 1880s and the 1920s called the *goldene medinah*, the "golden country," of opportunity, security, and prosperity. But if I had asked him, he would probably have smiled the beatific smile that sometimes appeared, like the sun breaking through a sky full of clouds, on his otherwise rather dour countenance, and shaken his head in disagreement. The smile would have betokened the appreciation he always accorded a clever remark (not excluding one that he was making himself), and the disagreement would have registered his rationalistic skepticism of any such idea. It would also have flowed from his awareness that even a playful analogy between the condition of the Jews of Spain in the fifteenth century and their position in the America of the 1950s was seriously flawed—and precisely because of the radically different role played by religion in their respective lives.

Mordecai M. Kaplan, the founder of Reconstructionism (originally an offshoot of the Conservative branch of American Judaism but eventually to become more radical in its repudiation of Orthodox tradition than the Reform branch), defined the Jewish religion as a "civilization," and though Cohen was not a Reconstructionist, his own conception had something in common with Kaplan's. Chances are that, if pressed, he would have used the term "Jewishness" rather than "Judaism," and "culture" rather than "civilization," signifying a shared history and a body of experience that had bred special habits of mind and being that were a highly valuable, and indeed indispensable, part of the Western heritage of which America had become the main custodian. (Not even Henry Luce of the *Time-Life* empire believed that this was "the American century," as he called it, more fervently than did Cohen.)

As such, the culture of Jewishness demanded to be preserved. Not because—as the theologian Emil L. Fackenheim would formulate the issue in a highly influential article that was to appear in

Commentary under my own editorship—failing to preserve it would give a "posthumous victory" to Hitler. To Cohen, the emphasis would have been on the consequences for *America* of this failure, which would rob the country of one of the pillars on which it rested, thereby leaving it weaker precisely at a moment when it needed all the strength it could muster in its struggle against Communist totalitarianism.

This idea contrasted sharply with the feelings toward their own religious heritage of the six or seven Jews (among them Frank Meyer, Marvin Liebman, Willi Schlamm, and Morrie Ryskind) who formed part of the conservative group that gathered around William F. Buckley, Jr. when he founded *National Review* in the mid-1950s. Most of them were ex-Communists who, according to the leading historian of American conservatism, George Nash, came increasingly to see religion as the bulwark of Western civilization in its struggle against Communism (at the basis of whose sins and crimes, in their view, was its "godlessness" and its opposition to all religion as what Marx derisively termed the "opiate of the people"). But Judaism, of which they all had a primitive conception as consisting of nothing but ritual, was not the religion to which they looked. Far from it: several of them wound up converting to Catholicism, and the others, without going all the way, became what might be called fellow-travelers of the Church, even to the point of attending mass. One of these latter, Frank Chodorov, wrote an essay entitled "How a Jew Came to God: An Intellectual Experience," which began with the sentence: "I am a Jew. Not that anyone cares about it, least of all myself."

The great exception in the *National Review* circle was Will Herberg. Like the others he was an ex-Communist but, traveling the route Cohen was independently trying to explore, Herberg embraced the faith of his fathers and went on to become a prominent Jewish theologian. He also became a contributor to *Commentary*, and in 1955, in his book *Protestant-Catholic-Jew*, he developed an argument very congenial to Cohen: that Judaism in America was now seen as embodying the same "spiritual values" as Christianity. In this sense, it had become a full partner in propagating "the American Creed." Indeed, Herberg declared, "being a Protestant, a Catholic or a Jew, is understood as the specific way, and increasingly perhaps the only way, of being an American and locating oneself in American society."

Though Cohen himself, and the magazine he edited, put much more stress on Jewish ethnicity and Jewish history than on religion, Herberg's thesis came very close to the point *Commentary* itself was trying to make, which was that the Jews of America—all of them and not just the intellectuals— *belonged* here, they belonged *in* and *to* America. They were not living in *galut*, the Diaspora, waiting to be brought home by the messiah or by David Ben-Gurion: they were home already. Certainly the "displaced persons" who had survived the Nazi concentration camps needed a refuge, and Palestine (still under the British mandate) perhaps could serve that need in some form. But the Zionist idea that this form had to be a sovereign Jewish state raised too many problems, among them the danger that American Jews might be subjected to charges of "dual loyalty"—ironically, just when they were finally learning that it was America that deserved their full loyalty.

Not, therefore, the Soviet Union, not a Jewish state in Palestine or some other place (there were those who once thought Uganda [!] might be a better location for such a state), but America: the country which had just put some sixteen million men under arms to defeat the worst enemy the Jewish people had ever encountered in their four-thousand-year history, and in which Jews had already begun to flourish and would go on prospering (though to an extent that not even Cohen would have been optimistic enough to foresee).

None of this is to imply that Elliot Cohen's *Commentary* was blind to the persistence of anti-Semitism in certain American quarters or the presence of discriminatory barriers to Jewish advancement. How could it be? It was common knowledge that restrictive quotas still limited the number of Jewish students who could be admitted into the most prestigious colleges and professional schools; that Jews were kept out of certain law firms and even virtually prevented from entering a whole profession like engineering; that Jews were barred from membership in many social clubs; and so on.

It hardly needs mentioning that *Commentary* was against all this. On the other hand, the magazine adopted a policy of calling as little attention as possible to anti-Semitic hate groups, on the theory (developed by the expert who was then calling the shots for its publisher, the American Jewish Committee, on how to defend against this threat) that the silent treatment was a more effective counter than outright confrontation. The result of this "quarantine" policy was that anyone whose information came only from *Commentary* would have thought that organizations devoted to spreading anti-Semitic propaganda were no longer active in the United States.

Paradoxically, however, if this impression was false in the strictest terms, it pointed to a deeper truth about the dimensions of the problem. It was a truth connected with the Holocaust, although this connection had not yet become directly evident. As the historian Tony Judt of New York University has described the situation in the immediate postwar years (a description for whose accuracy I can vouch on the basis of first-hand observation):

Most Americans (including most American Jews) had only the sketchiest notion of Hitler's war against the Jews. It was not until well into the 1960s that this began to change. It was then, and with gathering speed, that the Holocaust (not generally known as such until the mid-60s at the earliest) entered

American public life and went on to become a staple of enter-
tainment, moral education, electoral politics, media attention, comparative victimology, and foreign-policy debate.

Judt does not mention any of the books about the death camps
that came out shortly after the war, but then again all, or almost all,
were published in Europe and they were few and far between. Nor
was there more than a handful of articles, not even in *Commentary*,
let alone anywhere else. For the rest, Judt continues:

> In the years after 1945, the "displaced persons" of World War
> II (the term "survivors" was not yet in fashion) were not at the
> center of most people's attention, and the sufferings of the
> Jews among them did not attract special concern. . . . The pre-
> sentation and the reception of *The Diary of Anne Frank* (the
> book, the play, and the film) were indicative: if there were
> lessons, they were redemptive and universal. The fact that
> Anne was a Jew was almost incidental.* Those Jews who came
> to the United States in the post-war years (about 100,000
> arrived by 1951) certainly had a different tale to tell, but most
> people were not listening.

I would add that not even the newsreels showing the liberation
of the concentration camps with their mountains of Jewish
corpses, and the pitifully emaciated Jewish survivors who looked

---

*Not, however, to *Commentary*, which introduced the diary through an excerpt
before it was published in book form. But the people responsible for the adaptation of the book into a Broadway play and then a movie did everything they could
to "dejudaize" and "universalize" it. The novelist Meyer Levin, who wrote a competing version emphasizing its Jewishness, charged (with considerable justification) that these people—who included Lillian Hellman as adviser to the authors of
the adaptation, Albert and Frances Hackett—were motivated by a Communist-
inspired hostility to Jewish particularism.

like corpses themselves, were enough to prevent the continued maltreatment of these "displaced persons." Those who tried to make their way to Palestine were blocked by the British, and many wound up in new (though admittedly more benign) concentration camps on the island of Cyprus, while others who wanted to go elsewhere were not exactly welcomed with open arms.

Nevertheless, my own view is that what had befallen the Jews of Europe inculcated a subliminal lesson long before the emergence of the Holocaust as a major "staple" of American culture, both high and popular. The lesson was that anti-Semitism, even the relatively harmless genteel variety that enforced quotas against Jewish students or kept their parents from joining fashionable clubs or getting jobs in prestigious Wall Street law firms, could end in mass murder. Admittedly, it took a while for this lesson to penetrate certain thick or intransigently obdurate skulls, and even where it got through more quickly, it may well have done so in a less than fully conscious or fully formed shape.

This lag may explain why the barriers against Jews in America did not topple all at once in the years right after the end of the war. When I entered Columbia in 1946, it was under a 17 percent Jewish quota—at Harvard, it was somewhat higher and at Yale and Princeton somewhat lower—even if the university authorities refused to admit that this was their policy (just as, conversely, they would do after 1970 when, under the euphemism of "affirmative action," they would establish quotas of the opposite kind for blacks). Similar observations could be made about other areas of American life which Jews were discouraged by various means from entering.

Yet even before the penitential effect of the Holocaust had come into play, this was very far from the whole story. To begin with, the discriminatory barriers against Jews in America had never been as high or as unbreachable as those in other countries. Leaving aside restrictions in certain states that were hangovers from colonial times and that were in any event aimed primarily against Catholics, never were Jews who came to this country denied citizenship and the rights that went with it or the freedom to practice their own religion. George Washington was not being merely rhetorical when he wrote in his much-cited letter of 1790 to the Hebrew Congregation in Newport, Rhode Island:

> ... The Citizens of the United States of America have a right to applaud themselves for having given to mankind examples of an enlarged and liberal policy: a policy worthy of imitation. All possess alike liberty of conscience and immunities of citizenship. It is now no more that toleration is spoken of, as if it was by the indulgence of one class of people, that another enjoyed the exercise of their inherent and natural rights. For happily the Government of the United States, which gives to bigotry no sanction, to persecution no assistance requires only that they who live under its protection should demean themselves as good citizens, in giving it on all occasions their effectual support. ... May the Children of the Stock of Abraham, who dwell in this land, continue to merit and enjoy the good will of the other Inhabitants; while every one shall sit in safety under his own vine and figtree, and there shall be none to make him afraid ...

But even if Washington, a Virginian who not only sanctioned slavery but owned slaves himself, were being hypocritical in these lofty professions,* the hypocrisy did not touch upon the Jews. On the contrary, and for two reasons.

First was the very existence of Negro slavery. Virtually all the founding fathers knew it to be a sin and expected that a terrible punishment would some day be visited upon the country for it ("I

---

*I for one would defend him against the charge, though the issue is too complicated to deal with here.

tremble for my country," said another Virginian slave holder, Thomas Jefferson, "when I reflect that God is just"). In consequence, it was the blacks who would play the role in American society and in the American soul that the Jews had played, and would go on playing, for so many centuries in Europe. As Christian Europe was obsessed with the Jews, America was obsessed with the blacks—an obsession that in each place was made all the more poisonous by a bad conscience that no theological doctrine could completely assuage and no political rationalization entirely eradicate.

The second, and related, reason was that where the Jews were concerned, the Christians of America were very different from the Christians of Europe. All exceptions duly acknowledged—though they were not exactly plentiful—to the Christians of Europe, Protestant and Catholic alike, the Jews were doubly cursed: their ancestors had crucified Jesus, and they themselves continued to deny that he was the messiah for whom they had been waiting. Often this attitude led to massacres and expulsions (making a concrete reality out of the various versions of the myth of "the Wandering Jew"). But short of that, it served at the very least as the basis for denying the Jews any civil or political rights, and at the most for measures aimed at keeping them in a state of misery that would be the visible sign of their wickedness in rejecting Christ.*

Nothing could be further from this than the attitude toward the Jewish people held by the Puritans who were the first Christians to settle America and who set their stamp so firmly upon it. Far from looking upon the Jews as a people cursed, the Puritans identified with the Children of Israel. It would be an exaggeration to

---

*This was the policy even of some popes who opposed anti-Jewish violence.

say that they were philo- rather than anti-Semites, and an anachronism to conceive of them as precursors of the modern interreligious spirit. But it would be neither an exaggeration nor an anachronism to say that they felt a great affinity with the ancient Hebrews whom they knew so well from what they called the Old Testament, to which (again unlike the Europeans) they tended to be more attracted than they were to the New. As Edmund Wilson cogently summarized it in an article in *Commentary* that was subsequently reprinted in an expanded version in his book *A Piece of My Mind* (1956):

> When the Puritans came to America, they identified George III with Pharaoh and themselves with the Israelites in search of the Promised Land. They called their new country Canaan and talked continually of the Covenant they had made with God. . . . "The Christian church so-called," said a preacher in New Marlborough, Massachusetts, "is only a continuation and extension of the Jewish church." "If we keep this covenant," said [the Governor of Massachusetts, John] Winthrop, "we shall finde then the God of Israel is among us."

This tradition, Wilson added,

> came to life again—after a partial eclipse during the early eighteen hundreds—in the Abolitionist crusade against slavery that inspired so much of the ardor of the Federal forces in the Civil War. *The Battle Hymn of the Republic* comes straight out of the Biblical Prophets, and the Jehovah of the Old Testament takes the field again at the head of the Federal armies.

Which brings up the "little woman who wrote the book that started this great war," as Abraham Lincoln addressed the author of *Uncle Tom's Cabin* upon meeting her. For Harriet Beecher

Stowe was another product of the same tradition ("I think," she wrote, "no New Englander, brought up under the regime established by the Puritans, could really estimate how much of himself had actually been formed by [his] constant face-to-face intimacy with Hebrew literature"). Going even further, her husband Calvin, himself a scholar not only of the Hebrew Bible but even of the Talmud, habitually wore a skullcap and was referred to by her as "my old rabbi." Then there was the Harvard literary scholar Barrett Wendell, whom Wilson described as "the perfect type of old-fashioned snob in regard to every kind of American not of strictly Anglo-Saxon origins." Snob or not, Wendell admitted to believing that it was (in his own words) "wholly possible . . . that the Yankee Puritan, with all his Old Testament feeling, was really, without knowing it, largely Jewish in blood. There is in the Yankee nature much that would give color to the theory. . . ."

Having compiled these and other fascinating instances, Wilson went on to set them side-by-side with the outbursts of anti-Semitism, often very violent, that would nevertheless erupt from time to time on the highest levels of American culture. Ironically these grew precisely out of an updated version of the Puritans' identification with the Jews. Thus the writer John Jay Chapman and the poet and diplomat James Russell Lowell both began with a glorification of the Jews that, said Wilson, "passed suddenly into a neurotic anti-Semitism."

Lowell was an especially interesting case. According to a reporter who once interviewed him, he could speak of nothing but the Jews—

> their talent and versatility, and of the numbers who had been illustrious in literature, the learned professions, art, science, and even war, until by degrees, from being shut out of society and every honorable and desirable pursuit, they had gained prominent positions everywhere.

No wonder, as Wilson remarked, that Lowell should have developed "something of the state of mind that leads people to believe in the *Protocols of [the Elders of] Zion,* in a Jewish international conspiracy to dominate the civilized world."

Granting all this, and more, I would still maintain that even at its worst, anti-Semitism never went as deep in Christian America as it did in Christian Europe. Not only was it counterbalanced or undermined here, as never happened in Europe, by the strain of benevolent feeling toward the Jews that was brought over by the Puritans and that remained a force in the American psyche; anti-Semitism was further denied nourishment in the realm of ideas by the same "American Creed"—the belief that "all men are created equal and endowed by their Creator with certain inalienable rights"—that the Swedish sociologist Gunnar Myrdal, writing in 1944, argued must inexorably lead to the enfranchisement of the Negro and his full integration into American society. If the Negro was the object of a sick American obsession analogous in certain respects to the one prevailing in Europe toward the Jew, which therefore to some extent let the Jew off the hook here, the movement to win full civil rights for the Negro still benefited the Jew as well. Acting on the principle that "all bigotry is indivisible," Jewish organizations such as the American Jewish Committee and the Anti-Defamation League, whose purpose was to defend Jews against discrimination and defamation, joined enthusiastically in the civil-rights movement, of which individual Jews were for a long time leaders and funders.

But the "indivisibility" of bigotry was less self-evident than it seemed to those who endlessly repeated the mantra for so many years. This became clear when, in the 1960s, the tradition of black nationalism triumphed over the integrationist civil-rights movement with which it had always been at bitter odds. Pointing an accusatory finger at the very principle that Jewish organizations which had been founded (and were still being funded) to defend Jews came to invoke in justifying a greater concentration on the plight of the Negroes than that of the Jews themselves, the new "black" leaders who ousted their old "Negro" rivals accused the Jews of having supported the civil-rights movement only out of their own self-interest. And that was among the mildest of the charges they hurled.

Like the others, this one was false. Jewish support for the civil-rights movement flowed not primarily from a devious strategy of self-interest but from the liberalism to which the vast majority of American Jews were so tightly tied that hardly anything could shake them loose from its grip. Of course one might push the argument a step back and claim that Jewish liberalism itself stemmed from considerations of self-interest. If this were true, I myself would see nothing wrong with it. Indeed, I would regard it as the mark of a healthy self-respect. Unfortunately from my point of view, however, it was not true.

We know that it was not true from the fact that, unlike every other ethnic group, Jews (as the Republican party in New York would discover to its bewilderment whenever it put a Jew up against a non-Jewish Democrat) consistently voted for a Gentile running against a Jew if the former were perceived as more liberal than the latter. Even when Jews voted for a Jewish Republican, which occasionally happened, it would be a *liberal* Republican like Jacob Javits whose support for the civil-rights movement was as fervent as that of any Democrat. But an even more decisive refutation of the black charge was the much-quoted remark by the Jewish scholar Milton Himmelfarb that—again unlike all other ethnic groups, who tended to shift away from the Democrats and toward the Republicans as they became more prosperous—"Jews lived like Episcopalians and voted like Puerto Ricans."

The turn by blacks against their Jewish allies was not restricted to a moral denigration of this alliance. I have already referred to the battle between the teachers' union and a coalition of black radicals over control of the New York City public schools in 1967, which by a diabolical coincidence exploded in the same year the Six-Day War broke out in the Middle East. In response to these two unrelated events, the new breed of black leaders let loose a torrent of anti-Semitic filth.

Two typically noxious samples should suffice to give a whiff of this garbage. One, drawn from the school fight, was a poem written by a black participant and read on a left-wing radio station: "Hey little Jewboy / With your yarmulke on your head, / Hey little Jewboy / I wish you were dead." The other, concerning the Israeli victory in the Six-Day War, was a cartoon in the newsletter of SNCC (the Student Non-Violent Coordinating Commmittee, which had kept the name even after repudiating what it signified by advocating a new strategy of "taking up the gun"). This cartoon was planted in the midst of an analysis of the war in which the Palestinians and other Arabs were portrayed as dark-skinned victims of colonialist racism and the Israelis as spearheads of a counterrevolutionary American imperialism. To illustrate, the cartoonist depicted General Moshe Dayan, who had led the Israeli forces to victory, in the uniform of a Nazi tank commander with a swastika on his arm and dollar signs for eyes.

Disgusting as this kind of stuff was in its own right, the shock of it was intensified by the fact that such blatant expressions of anti-Semitism had become very rare in America since the end of the Second World War. To the degree that it still existed—as of course it did in certain quarters—it had been marginalized to the point of being rendered invisible within the mainstream. And here I come back once more to why I believe something is missing from Tony Judt's otherwise accurate contention that the Holocaust did not become a factor in the American consciousness until the early 1960s.

· · ·

To recapitulate my own take on this question: while no one, including the Jews themselves, wanted to talk about and dwell on it at first, the knowledge that hostility toward the Jews could lead to mass murder had enough unconscious or subliminal influence to banish the open expression of anti-Semitic feelings and ideas from public discourse. Anyone who had such ideas or harbored such feelings could only bring them out into the open at the cost of being, in effect, excommunicated from respectable society.

This was especially so—and well before the 1960s—on the Right. Having in the past been more hospitable to anti-Semitism than the Left, and hence sensitive to the political dangers of being associated, however distantly, with the Nazis, right-wing intellectuals and politicians made a determined effort to demonstrate that they would no longer tolerate anti-Semitism in their midst. This was what William F. Buckley, Jr. did when he founded *National Review* in the mid-1950s, and also what induced Senator Joseph R. McCarthy to hire two young Jews, Roy Cohn and G. David Schine, as his principal assistants.

It was because this taboo against the open expression of anti-Semitism had been so effective that the breaking of it by the black radicals of the late 1960s acquired even greater shock value than it would have had strictly on its own. More ominous yet was the response of what the black radicals themselves liked to call "the white power establishment." Partly out of the fear of black violence bred by the urban riots of the mid-1960s, and partly because the establishment was still so condescending toward blacks that it could not bring itself to take their anti-Semitic outbursts seriously, these outbursts were tolerated and even apologized for as an "understandable" product of the black community's resentment of its former dependence on the Jews and its salutary new wish to control its own destiny. Far from being ostracized or punished with neglect, as any white anti-Semite would have been, black anti-Semites (in a new version of the protection rackets of old) were now given grants by institutions like the Ford Foundation and treated by city officials as the legitimate spokesmen of their people.

In New York, the shift in attitudes among both blacks and whites more or less coincided with the mayoralty of John V. Lindsay (1965–1973), a liberal Republican who ultimately made an honest man out of himself by becoming a liberal Democrat. But probably just as significant was the accession in that same era of McGeorge Bundy to the presidency of the Ford Foundation in New York. Before his appointment to this job, Bundy had been national security adviser to Presidents John F. Kennedy and Lyndon B. Johnson, and had played a key role in the American decision first to intervene in Vietnam and then to escalate our involvement. But by the time he left the waning Johnson administration, Bundy had evidently come to believe that it had been a mistake to resist the Communist Vietcong in the first place. On the basis of the policy he immediately adopted as the new president of the Ford Foundation, I used to speculate jokingly that no sooner had he arrived there than he summoned his staff and demanded that they bring him the Vietcong. The Vietcong? In New York? At so uncomprehending a reaction, as I imagined the scene, a derisive sneer formed on the lips of this famously arrogant New England patrician who knew as much about New York as he had about Vietnam when he plunged into it. "I mean the black radicals, the militants," I could hear him snarling at his underlings. "Get them up here, because this time, instead of fighting them, we're going to give them all grants."

Bad as it was from every possible angle, to me this indulgence toward anti-Semitism among blacks cast a contrasting retrospective light on the extent to which the *goldene medinah* over the previous two decades had produced, if not another Golden Age of Jewish culture such as had occurred in medieval Spain, then a Golden Age of Jewish security such as had never been experienced anywhere in the two thousand years of the Diaspora. In addition to the strict, if informal, enforcement of the taboo against the open expression of anti-Semitism, the discriminatory barriers that had previously been erected against Jewish economic and social advancement also finally began falling one after another.

Admittedly, some of this progress came about as the result of less lofty considerations than would have been dictated by George Washington's letter to the Jews of Newport or the "American Creed," or by the penitential influence of the Holocaust. Restrictive quotas were abolished in the major universities, for example, only after 1957, and mainly because the Soviet launching of Sputnik into space persuaded the powers-that-were that the American national interest demanded an improvement in scientific training. This required adopting a strict merit system in admissions policies, which in turn entailed the doing-away with any measures that might keep bright students out only because they were Jews.

Even if the motive was less than fully pure, however, discrimination against Jewish applicants became a thing of the past. So too did discrimination in other sectors of American life, including professions, businesses, corporate and philanthropic boards, private clubs, residential areas, and so on. In line with Will Herberg's analysis in *Protestant-Catholic-Jew*, it was now customary—even obligatory—to include a rabbi along with a minister and a priest at public ceremonial occasions. And in politics, more and more Jewish candidates were running and winning, even—through a kind of reverse payback for the readiness noted above of Jews to vote for a Gentile running against "one of their own" in jurisdictions where they were a preponderant group—in districts where few Jewish voters could be found.

So prominent did the presence of Jews become in American society (just as James Russell Lowell had prophesied—and feared—would happen) that in spite of being less than 3 percent of the population, they would cease being classified as a minority. But this occurred only when in the 1970s the word "minority" would stop being used to denominate a relative number. Instead it would become a generic euphemism for blacks and other groups (including, to what should have been everyone's befuddlement, women, since they actually constituted a numerical *majority* of the population as a whole) who were deemed not to have received their "fair share" of wealth or income or status. On this score alone, they were accorded the status of victims who deserved special compensatory treatment. However, in the absence of any laws resembling the "Jim Crow" legislation that had once existed against blacks, their condition had to be blamed on the hidden and more insidious operations of unconscious prejudices like racism or sexism, now defined more broadly than ever before to stigmatize previously acceptable language or behavior.

Furthermore, a new theory was designed to answer the question of why the beneficiaries of various civil-rights acts banning discrimination in many different forms and in many different social venues should still be deemed victims of discrimination. As applied to blacks, this theory was "institutional racism," which held that racism had been so inextricably built into the "system" that it operated even when the white individuals in charge were not themselves racists (on the doubtful assumption that any such individuals actually existed).

Women, for their part, invented the concept of "the glass ceiling," which was an invisible limit set by sexism to their advancement. Yet the very need to create such a concept was itself a measure of how far they had gone in achieving the economic goals of the women's liberation movement. What remained hanging was the question of whether these gains (which included greater sexual freedom as well as expanded opportunity in the marketplace) were worth the price they exacted in social dislocation and individual confusion among women themselves and the men with whom they were inescapably and ineluctably entangled, not to mention the children they either did or did not bear.

A decade or so after women's lib came the gay-rights movement, which tried, and with considerable success, to include homosexuals as one of the victimized groups. From one angle, this movement had a better case than blacks and women, since unlike them, homosexuals still confronted laws in a number of states criminalizing their sexual behavior and/or forbidding same-sex marriages. "Sexual orientation," however, raised issues very different from skin color or gender, which was why political support for the gay-rights movement was harder to build than it had been for blacks and women. When in 1999 the sociologist Alan Wolfe studied American attitudes on these matters, he discovered that "live and let live" had become the rule on the sexual mores that had been at the center of the "culture wars"—except where homosexuals were concerned. As the twentieth century was coming to an end, most Americans were willing to tolerate homosexuality, but they were unwilling to give it the stamp of approval that was the true objective of the gay-rights movement, and they were still against same-sex marriage.

B ut all that is yet another (though related) story than the one I am trying to tell here. In resuming it now after this long series of digressions and asides, I wish to stress the point I started with when I suggested that a deeper truth lay behind Elliot Cohen's judgment that anti-Semitism was on the wane in America, and that its persistence was more a symptom of atavism than a sign of the present or a portent for the future.

Certainly my own experience bore this out. When, on December 16, 1955, the very next day after being discharged from my two-year hitch in the army, I went to work at *Commentary* as an assistant editor, I was just approaching my twenty-sixth birthday, and never had being Jewish created any difficulties for me. It had not prevented me from being offered those scholarships to two major Ivy League colleges; and it had not prevented me from winning those fellowships to Cambridge.

At Columbia, the only hint—and a hint was all it was—of anti-Semitism I ever ran into came in a course on Chaucer given by

Professor Raymond Weaver that I took as a sophomore. We had just read in *The Canterbury Tales* the story of Hugh of Lincoln (which was about a Christian child murdered by Jews so that they could use his blood in making matzos on Passover*), and when Weaver asked in a rather belligerent voice whether anyone in the class thought that it showed Chaucer to be anti-Semitic, I raised my hand. Glancing around, Weaver noted that mine was the only hand in the air, and he glared at me for a few endless seconds before growling in a tone that combined satisfaction with the utmost scorn, "Don't you know that Chaucer never even *saw* a Jew?" As it happened, I did know that, being well aware that the Jews had been expelled from England before Chaucer's time and were not readmitted until the seventeenth century under (significantly) the Puritan Oliver Cromwell. Weaver would allow me neither to defend my position nor to affirm that I did not blame Chaucer for being a man of his time, and for the rest of that term he treated me with unmistakable hostility. But this incident was so inconsequential that Weaver did not even punish me with a bad grade in the course.

Even at Cambridge, I encountered no anti-Semitism. I suppose if I had been more sensitive on this score, I would have felt uncomfortable, or discriminated against, by the recitation before every meal in my college (which, by a wonderful and—to me—glorious coincidence, Chaucer himself had attended) of a short Latin grace ending with the words "*per Christum Dominum nostrum.*" But even though I understood what those words meant, I was no more bothered by them than I had been by the singing of the incomprehensible lyrics of "Holy, Holy, Holy" in elementary school; and no one objected, or even seemed to notice, when I sat silent during the recitation of grace. Jews in England—even those who had lived

---

*The "blood libel" was a staple of medieval anti-Semitism, and in spreading it here, Chaucer was using a historical case in which the Jews had been accused of murdering the child, who was later canonized by the Church.

there for centuries—tended in those days to be considered slightly foreign, and Jews who actually were foreign got subsumed into the old saying, "The wogs begin at Calais."* Unless, that is, they were Americans, in which case it was that part of their identity that became the target of animosity and not their Jewishness.

Indeed, the only consequence being Jewish had for me at Cambridge was entirely benign. About a week before the graduating ceremonies, I was summoned into the office of the Senior Tutor, the college official in charge of the event. "Mr. Podhoretz, you're Jewish, aren't you?" he asked. "Yes sir," I admitted, "I am." Well, he said, as a vestigial remnant of the monastic origins of the older Cambridge colleges like Clare (founded in 1326), degrees were conferred through a laying-on of hands by the vice-chancellor of the university on the head of the kneeling candidate, and "in the name of the Father, the Son, and the Holy Ghost." Did I have any objection to that? After pausing to think about it for a second or two, I decided that I did. No problem, he replied. If I were willing to kneel before the Vice-Chancellor's throne (which I was), he could award me the degree "in the name of God" (*in nomine Dei*) alone. This, the Senior Tutor explained, was often done with Hindu students from India. And so it was done with this Jewish student from America.

The same situation obtained during my two years in the army. There, the only times my Jewishness ever came up was when someone—usually one of my friends from the rural South—who had never or only rarely met a Jew would ask me about it out of curiosity. But never, not once, either when I was stationed in the States or in Germany, did being Jewish create any problems for me.

After my discharge, deciding that I would rather work at *Com-*

---

*The word "wog," of course, originated in the days of the British empire as a sarcastic acronym for "worthy Oriental gentleman."

mentary than resume my studies toward a Ph.D., I took the place in the American intellectual community that I would occupy on various levels and in one way or another for the rest of my life. From then until the situation began changing in 1967, it became clearer and clearer to me that Jewishness had been transformed from the (relatively mild, as compared with the situation in Europe) disability it had been in earlier generations into a positive advantage.

The most telling symptom of this development was not so much the toppling I described above of one discriminatory barrier after another. Even more significant was the enormous interest being shown in Jewish writers dealing with the Jewish experience. I say that this was more telling and significant because historically the arts, and especially literature, had been harder for Jews to penetrate than almost any other area of the national life. To the extent that they succeeded in breaking through, it was as "non-Jewish Jews," or thoroughly assimilated writers whose material had nothing visibly Jewish about it; and even then, the very fact that they were Jewish (as in Berlin and Vienna in the 1920s) aroused tremendous resentment over what was considered an alien invasion of the culture.

This was truer of Europe than America, where—in yet another indication that anti-Semitism was much stronger there than here—no comparable resentment was provoked by writers of Jewish origin so long as they had abandoned any trace of Jewish particularism. Yet even in America, any Jewish writer unwilling to pay this price was almost certain to be ignored. The outstanding case in point was Henry Roth's *Call It Sleep*—a novel applying the literary techniques James Joyce had used in evoking Dublin to a story about an immigrant Jewish family on the Lower East Side of New York. Recognized by a few critics even upon its original publication in 1933 as the masterpiece it is now universally acknowledged to be, *Call It Sleep* still disappeared off the face of the literary earth (and so for many long years did its author).

What happened to Ludwig Lewisohn was equally revealing, if from another direction. Unlike Roth, Lewisohn had paid the necessary entry fee into the mainstream, and in the 1920s, when he was still a "non-Jewish Jew," his novels were widely celebrated and read. But (to borrow Heine's sardonic image of the rewards of conversion to Christianity and applying it to the less drastic context of assimilation) Lewisohn's "passport" was revoked when he underwent a conversion to Zionism and turned into a passionate advocate of Jewish identification. From that moment on, he became a virtual non-person in the American literary world.

Nor was it any different with literary scholarship and criticism. As late as the late 1930s, the English department at my future alma mater resisted awarding tenure to Lionel Trilling on the ground that, being Jewish, he was not deeply enough rooted in Anglo-Saxon culture to teach its literature to the young. Apart from being wrong (just as Richard Wagner had been wrong in constructing a similar argument to demonstrate that Jews were unable to write great music and were only capable of performing it*), this idea was a joke as applied to Trilling in particular, whose roots were planted far more firmly in the soil of English and American literature than in anything Jewish.

By the time I joined the editorial staff of *Commentary*, Trilling had become one of the leading literary critics in America, along with Jews like Alfred Kazin and Irving Howe; Jewish poets like Delmore Schwartz and Karl Shapiro—with Allen Ginsberg waiting in the wings—had emerged into the limelight; and Jewish novelists like Saul Bellow and Bernard Malamud were in the process

---

*This explains why, violently anti-Semitic though he had by then become, Wagner could still choose a Jew to conduct the premiere of his last opera, *Parsifal*, itself a work in which some commentators find his hatred of Jews reflected. Why the Jewish conductor accepted the assignment is another matter.

of displacing the Southerners who had been at the center of the action for some years now. Soon they would be joined by Philip Roth—not only no relation to Henry but destined for a career that would take the very opposite course from the older novelist's in terms both of productivity and of commercial success—and a host of lesser lights whose books about growing up and being Jewish in America were already becoming all the rage. With the always stark exception of Norman Mailer, other Jewish writers who had previously shown no interest in their background also got caught up in this new fashion—so much so that I used to quip that if Nathanael West had come along in the 1950s instead of the 1930s and had been born with that name, he might have changed it to Nathan Weinstein instead of the other way around. In addition, he might have written about being Jewish instead of almost ostentatiously ignoring that part of his life in the four novels he managed to produce before being killed in an automobile accident in 1940 at the age of thirty-seven.

I incorporated this quip about West né Weinstein into a lecture I used to be invited regularly to give at universities about the rise of the American Jewish novelist. In that same lecture, I also quoted two interesting complaints about this phenomenon. The first came from Truman Capote, one of the Southerners who felt displaced. In an interview with *Playboy*, Capote charged that a "Jewish mafia" had taken control of "much of the literary scene through the influence of the quarterlies and intellectual magazines." He then shifted into high gear:

> All these publications are Jewish-dominated and this particular coterie employs them to make or break writers by advancing or withholding attention. . . . Bernard Malamud and Saul Bellow and Philip Roth and Isaac Bashevis Singer and Norman Mailer are all fine writers but they're not the *only* writers in the country, as the Jewish mafia would have us believe. I could give you a list of excellent writers . . . ; the odds are you

haven't heard of most of them for the simple reason that the Jewish mafia has systematically frozen them out of the literary scene.

A similar complaint was lodged by Gore Vidal, who felt displaced not as a Southerner but as a WASP. He too alleged that the literary world had fallen under the domination of a Jewish establishment of critics and editors which made room on the list of the important novelists of his own generation only for an occasional "O.K. Goy" like himself.

The great irony was that the Jewish editors and critics who were supposedly pushing and promoting Jewish novelists and poets in this way were in reality their harshest, and often their only, critics. Nor was it even remotely accurate that, except for an occasional "O.K. Goy," a writer had to be Jewish in order to get himself noticed. Besides Capote and Vidal themselves, who were hardly starving for attention, there were such widely read and discussed novelists as William Styron, John Updike, John Cheever, James Jones, Flannery O'Connor, Ralph Ellison, and James Baldwin; and poets like Wallace Stevens, Robert Lowell, John Berryman, Theodore Roethke, Randall Jarrell, Elizabeth Bishop, Marianne Moore, and Sylvia Plath were both famous and admired. Adding to the irony, all these writers were treated with much greater tenderness by critics like Robert Penn Warren, Allen Tate, and Cleanth Brooks than their Jewish contemporaries could generally expect from such Jewish critics as Trilling, Howe, Philip Rahv, or, for that matter, me.

Here, then (and predating the eruption of anti-Semitism among blacks in 1967), was the first appearance in America of the same resentment over Jewish "dominance" of the national culture that had contributed greatly to the spread of anti-Semitism in Berlin and Vienna in the 1920s and that had thrown another crucial ingredient into the witches' brew from which Nazism drank deep and grew strong.

Yet even while sounding a faint alarm over this development

and its dangers, I did not see in it any evidence of a new wave of anti-Semitism. On the contrary, I interpreted it as a measure of how effective the taboo against the frank public voicing of anti-Semitic ideas or feelings had become since 1945. Because of this taboo, Capote and Vidal, like almost everyone else in America, were entirely unfamiliar with the standard canards of anti-Semitic tradition; and it was this very ignorance that emboldened them to spread an idea that they would have shunned or been ashamed of embracing if they had been aware of its history and pedigree. I still think this was true of Capote, but to my sorrow, I eventually learned how wrong I had been in exonerating Vidal, who did indeed turn out to be an anti-Semite.*

But like black anti-Semitism, the mutation that would be exploited by Vidal lay in the relatively distant future. In the meantime, the conditions that began manifesting themselves right after the war and then gathered steam and increasing force in the 1950s clearly demonstrated that I was not the only Jew who had found a home, and felt fully at home, in America.

The love affair I had been having with this country since childhood accordingly became more intense than ever. Why then should it have run just at that moment into a rocky patch? Looking back on those ardent youthful years from my present perspective as a septuagenarian who has long since settled into a steadier and more steadfast love, I detect a paradox in my surrender to some of the temptations to infidelity that began presenting themselves to me in the late 1950s.

The paradox was this: it was only because I had become so sure of myself as an American that I now thought nothing of criticizing or even attacking the country for its imperfections. Of course,

---

*See footnote, page 50.

there were always scads of people who did this without being sure of themselves as Americans—who, in fact, did it precisely *because* they were personally aggrieved at being ignored or denied respect (if they were artists or intellectuals who had "never met a payroll") or excluded (if they were of recent immigrant stock) or dispossessed (if they were of old patrician stock). All these marginalized groups avenged themselves by staging ideological guerrilla attacks from the sidelines to which they had been consigned, or the "bohemian" sanctuaries in which they found refuge, or the foreign countries to which they expatriated themselves.

Yet unlike these people, I and a fair number of my contemporaries had gone (as someone called it) "beyond alienation." Which meant that we differed from the generations that had come before in another respect. For all their railing and ranting, and for all the bravado with which (like the Communists during the Third Period of the 1920s and early 1930s and the Trotskyists in the early 1940s) they might speak of making a revolution against America, or (like Edmund Wilson at the start of the Great Depression) of ceasing to acquiesce in the "triumph of the businessman" and to take this country back from him and restore it to its rightful rulers (themselves, as spokesmen for the working class), most of the time they knew in their hearts that they were only addressing one another and they did not really expect to be heard either by the dominant forces of society or by the "masses."*

This was how I too saw things when I myself started embracing radical ideas in my writings and then, upon becoming the chief ed-

---

*In his rebuttal to Clement Greenberg and Dwight Macdonald's "Ten Propositions on the War," which I have already discussed in Part Two, Philip Rahv, who was capable of being more realistic about politics than many of his colleagues, made this clear: "Speaking for no movement, no party, certainly not for the working class, not even for any influential grouping of intellectuals, the authors of the 'Ten Propositions' nevertheless write as if they are backed up by masses of people. . . ." The same point is illustrated so perfectly by an anecdote I once heard that

itor of *Commentary* in 1960, dedicated the magazine to their development and propagation. I had no illusions about the "masses,"
but to my own initial astonishment, I soon discovered that I *was*
being heard by some of the elites, and that the attacks being
launched by *Commentary* were getting through to them loud and
clear—indeed, all the way to the White House.

The first indication I had of this came when one of President
John F. Kennedy's assistants complained about *Commentary*, which
had been attacking the administration from the Left both on domestic and foreign policy, to a delegation from the American Jewish Committee. The nonplussed AJC leaders, most of whom in
truth hardly ever read *Commentary*, responded by disclaiming any
responsibility for what appeared in its pages, and by explaining
that the magazine enjoyed complete editorial independence. This
was the literal truth, but it was a truth nearly impossible for the
kind of people surrounding Kennedy to believe. Hardened pols
that they were, they took it for granted that he who pays the piper
calls the tune.

When the AJC delegation returned to New York, I was summoned to a meeting and told that I was jeopardizing the organization's relations with the White House. Would I not consider the
harm this could do and agree to go a little easier? I said that this
was out of the question and offered my resignation. But being men
who understood the importance of the principle of editorial independence, and who in the end always proved willing to pay the
price for it, they declined either to fire me or to let me resign.

I have often told it before in dealing with this whole question. Some time in the
1930s, Harold Rosenberg, a New York intellectual who, like Greenberg, took the
whole world as his province but would later become best known as an art critic,
spotted the very abstruse literary theorist Kenneth Burke marching in a May Day
parade and waving a sign reading "WE WRITE FOR THE WORKERS!" "Kenneth,"
Rosenberg shouted as he watched Burke strut by, "*you* write for the workers?" To
which Burke shot back, "It's an ambiguity on the preposition 'for'!"

They therefore confined themselves to baleful shrugs of helplessness in the face of the uncontrollable young firebrand they had been imprudent enough to hire.

Nor was this echo from high places the only indication that I and the writers I had sought out as collaborators in building a new radicalism were being heard. In 1960, we regarded ourselves, and indeed were, only a small band of brothers, but—again to my initial astonishment—the ideas we had been shaping and disseminating spread faster and further than I had ever dreamed possible. Within five years—that is, by 1965—these ideas had become dominant in the universities and were on their way to achieving the same position in the major media. Most incredible of all, by 1972, they had actually taken over the Democratic party behind the candidacy of George McGovern.

I might have been expected to regard this as a vindication and a triumph, but the trouble was that something had gone terribly wrong with the new radicalism on its way up. In explaining his own disaffection from it, one of my then closest collaborators, the sociologist Nathan Glazer, remarked in passing that he himself had been only "a mild radical" to begin with. But even though he and I agreed on almost everything during that period, his description of himself was not quite a good fit for me. I had always tended to be more passionate or, if you like, hot-headed than Glazer about the issues on which we saw eye to eye. And on top of this temperamental difference was the utopianism that had driven me into radicalism in the first place, and that never exerted the same influence over him, if it had had any impact on him at all.

It was this utopian strain in my thinking and in my emotions that made my radicalism more fervent than his. In 1960, I was convinced that if only the United States had the will, the cold war and the "arms race" could be ended; that both the problems of race and those of poverty could be solved; that a new ethos stressing cooperation over competition could be formed—and with no ill effects on the economy; that a culture could be created in which every individual would have an opportunity to fulfill his own best potentialities, whatever they might be; that a new educational system could be established that would encourage this development to grow; that the relations between men and women, both generally and in the sexual domain in particular, could be loosened and liberated without destructive consequences for marriage or the rearing of children; and so on and on and on into the blinding visions of the utopian imagination. One more point: I was also convinced that all this could be done through reforms "within the system" and without revolutionary violence.

Obviously such a program implied a vast dissatisfaction with America as it then existed and really was. It bore, as I see now, the seeds of the anti-Americanism by which I would later be repelled. But it simultaneously embodied a limitless faith in the perfectibility of this country, and as such did not force the breakup of my love affair with it. I might clarify the point by an analogy with a love affair between two individuals in which one is pressing the other to change but that goes on even if the attempt is only partially successful, or has unintended and unwelcome consequences.

But let me be more concrete by talking a bit about two of the major issues of the 1960s, Vietnam and race.

In both cases, I began by taking positions that were scarcely distinguishable from those of my fellow radicals, of whom, to stress it again, there were then very few. But before long, and as their numbers grew, differences began surfacing. At first, as compared with the main points on which we all agreed (being against the American role in the war, and being convinced that the old civil-rights movement had run its course and that a 180-degree change in direction was needed), such differences did not seem all that large. But as I look back, I see what I did not perceive then: that they were early warning signs of the break that would occur by the end of the decade. In hindsight, it even becomes evident that I was from the word go, if largely unconsciously, already resisting the anti-American logic of the perspective I shared with my fellow radicals—a logic that (as with utopianism) most of them would prove only too happy to accept.

As to Vietnam, I was among the very earliest opponents of American intervention, on the ground that it was "the wrong war in the wrong place at the wrong time." It was General Maxwell Taylor who coined the phrase, but it was Hans J. Morgenthau, then perhaps the best-known theorist of the school of *Realpolitik* (or, in non-Germanic terminology, realism) in foreign affairs, who became its leading exponent. Under Morgenthau's tutelage, utopian though I was, I adopted his essentially anti-utopian position on Vietnam as my own, both by running him regularly in *Commentary* and by writing pieces of my own roughly reflecting the same point of view, at least with regard to that particular issue.

To appreciate the full significance of this position, and why it led me into so much conflict with my fellow radicals (and ultimately with Morgenthau himself when even *he* went over to them), it has to be set beside the competing analysis that gradually developed on the Left as our involvement in Vietnam deepened and as the number of opponents grew. In that alternative view, the American intervention in Vietnam was not a mistaken extension to Asia of the strategy of containment that had worked so well in holding the Soviet Union back in Europe; it was a criminal act of imperialism aimed at suppressing the legitimate national aspirations of a downtrodden dark-skinned people. It was the "wrong war" not because it was a wasteful and imprudent use of American power but because it was morally evil; it was the "wrong place" not because it was a foolishly chosen political and military field on which to hold the line against the spread of Communism, but because the fight being conducted by the Communists there was a fight for freedom that deserved our sympathy, not our opposition; and it was the "wrong time" not because conditions in the United States were unfavorable to the building of support for such a war, but because *any* time was the wrong time for such a war. As the American intervention widened and escalated, the way the war was conducted also came to be stigmatized as involving atrocities, illegal uses of force, and even a secret campaign of genocide.*

It was with the escalation of the war in the mid-1960s that Morgenthau himself underwent his startling conversion to the radical position on Vietnam and took to denouncing the American role in moralistic terms that, besides being hysterically off the mark in their relation to the facts, violated in every respect the realist perspective on foreign policy with which he had always been identified. But I refused to go along with him, or with those of my friends who also moved into that camp. For the purposes of propaganda and public relations, most of them pretended to favor a negotiated settlement rather than a Communist victory, though others who were less concerned about driving away potential support in "Middle America" made no secret of their hope for a Communist takeover of the whole of Vietnam. Some—notably Norman Mailer—were frank to admit that they yearned for an American defeat and most especially the humiliation it would carry with it.

I too advocated a negotiated settlement, one that would bring about an American withdrawal and yet allow South Vietnam to exist as a non-Communist country that, with any luck, and under conditions of peace, would develop into a real democracy. But unlike those of my friends who for prudential political reasons pretended to favor the same outcome, I really meant it; and I was still enough of a utopian, or anyway unrealistic enough, to imagine that such a settlement could be reached with what Henry Kissinger, even while negotiating with them, aptly characterized as "the icy totalitarians of the North." In still sharper contrast to my

---

*The charge of genocide was especially bizarre, since the population of North Vietnam, which we were allegedly trying to wipe out, actually *grew* during the course of the war. But—see the footnote on page 88—the other charges were also either wildly exaggerated or completely false.

friends, I was also disgusted by the gleeful anticipation not just of a North Vietnamese victory but of an American humiliation. Never having believed that America had committed a crime in entering the war, nor in its conduct of it, I did not share Norman Mailer's wish to see this country humiliated.

It was only toward the end, when a Communist victory seemed certain and threats were being made by the Nixon administration to resume large-scale bombing of the North, that I finally gave up and wrote a piece in which I said that an American defeat would be preferable to a return of the B-52 bombers over North Vietnam. But I said it reluctantly, and with a heavy heart, and with no illusions about the "bloodbath" and the other horrors that were sure to follow the conquest of the South by the Communists of the North. And I said it only because I had come to the conclusion that the sole alternative to a defeat was now a continuation of the war, and that such a continuation would be a futile exercise in pointless destruction.

What I only faintly perceived then, but what became blazingly vivid to me later, was that my love of America had remained strong enough to withstand more than a dozen years of deep disapproval over its ever-escalating involvement in a war that I thought it should never have entered. It had also survived a close association during those years with people whose own love of America (to the extent that they had ever felt any at all; and if they had, it was for an America that existed only in their heads, not for the one in the real world in which we all lived) had turned into such sheer hatred that they did not hesitate to compare this country to Nazi Germany. By the early 1970s, the invocation of this comparison had become so promiscuous that it had almost—not quite, but almost—lost the power to shock. But the first time I heard it, in the mid-1960s, coming from the lips of a close friend with whom I was having dinner at an expensive restaurant, I was so outraged that I lost my temper and stormed out of the place. As I left, I shouted at him in a very loud voice that if I felt that way, I would consider emigration the only honorable course. He responded with a smirk and cut himself another slice of steak.

Comparing "Amerika" with Nazi Germany soon also became commonplace in discussions of race. Here, as I have noted, it began with Israel, cast as a surrogate of the United States, after the Six-Day War of 1967. But the first time I can recall seeing it applied directly to America itself was not during a meal in a restaurant; it was during a march headed toward Harlem and led by a bus with the word "Auschwitz" printed in the destination panel on the front. Again my disgust knew no bounds.

It is demeaning to flash my credentials as a venerable supporter of the civil-rights movement. And yet I fear I have to do so here if only to show that my disgust over that march did not betoken any failure of sympathy with the plight of the black community, and especially its poorest members.

So: in my own writings—especially the notorious essay "My Negro Problem—and Ours" that appeared in *Commentary* in 1963—and in articles by others than ran regularly in the magazine, I had thrown such weight as I had behind the very first stirrings of a turn in the black community away from the leaders whose strategic goal was integration and whose tactics consisted of pushing for legislation and appealing to the courts. In particular, I offered sympathy and space to the young radicals who were attacking these leaders for being too slow and too limited in their objectives, and who called for a new movement aiming at "Black Power."

Even the one black integrationist who continued writing regularly for *Commentary*, Bayard Rustin, was a radical. For unlike the liberal integrationists Roy Wilkins of the NAACP and Whitney Young of the Urban League, Rustin was also a socialist. This meant that he agreed with the new black nationalists in thinking that integration by itself would not solve the economic problems of the black community. As an integrationist, however, he parted company with the nationalists in their advocacy of separatism, and as a follower of Gandhi's doctrine of nonviolence, neither could he countenance their increasingly open summons to armed insurrection. His own solution was not revolution, which he was against in principle and also considered totally unrealistic as a practical matter. Rather he pushed for something like a domestic version of the Marshall plan, which had been so successful in rebuilding a wartorn Europe, and which, he thought, was a necessary addition to the civil-rights legislation that he also supported.

Because of his opposition to violence, Rustin went around during the riots that erupted all over the country in the mid-1960s issuing pleas for calm at considerable risk to his own safety. Yet he could still write an article, which (once more a blush of embarrassment comes to my cheeks) I encouraged him to do, and which I then published in *Commentary*, designating those riots as a "manifesto." Without exactly justifying or apologizing for them, he (and I) still interpreted such outbreaks as evidence that much more—namely, his own domestic Marshall plan—was needed to assuage the anger and alleviate the plight of the black poor than the civil-rights acts of 1964 and 1965.

Still, Bayard Rustin—for all that he had spent his share of time in jail for being a conscientious objector during World War II, for participating in "illegal" demonstrations in the South, and (though this was covered up) for homosexual solicitation—was no hater of America. And this too separated him from the radical nationalists. Nor (unlike many white liberals) could Rustin tolerate the anti-Semitism that invariably traveled in tandem with the anti-Americanism, and to whose eruption into public view in 1967 he had the same reaction as I did. So far as we were both concerned, black anti-Semitism was still anti-Semitism, and anyone who justified or apologized for it was justifying and apologizing for anti-Semitism. Of this he would have no more to do than I myself would. And both of us absolutely rejected the idea—which had become pervasive among radicals in the late 1960s—that America was too rotten to be saved by anything short of a revolution.

As with Vietnam, then, on this other major issue of the 1960s my love affair with America survived a long bout of infidelity. D. H. Lawrence (whom I regarded in my youth as the greatest contemporary British novelist) also wrote a good deal of verse, and one of the volumes he produced was about a crisis in his marriage that was finally resolved. The title poem of that book, "Look! We Have Come Through!," struck me then as almost eerily applicable to my love affair with America, which was rekindled toward the end of the 1960s and became more passionate than it ever had been before.

It did not happen all at once. There was a process and it stretched over a number of years. Triggered by my recoil from the anti-Americanism of the Left (which metastasized beyond Vietnam and race and spread though the entire body politic), it required time and reflection before it could evolve into something more positive and find more solid grounding in a new intellectual setting. It also required repentance: I could only "come through" fully by first acknowledging my own responsibility for the spread of what I now deplored and even loathed. That, in turn, involved a painful examination of what it was in the ideas I had held and helped to disseminate that could have given birth to the monsters I now hated and feared.

What made this especially difficult was that my own version of these ideas had never been tainted with an actual *hatred* of America. How then could they have played so large a part in the breeding and the spread of this—as I now saw it—morbid and dangerous pathology? The answer I kept coming back to time after time in questioning myself was that the fault lay in the utopian character of my radical viewpoint. As little regard as I had for

Marxism, I had to admit that there was a lot to be said for its contemptuous attitude toward utopianism.

Utopianism might begin, as it had done in my own case, innocently enough with the belief that the status quo left much to be desired, and that, guided by a vision of a better world, it could be vastly improved, even unto perfection. In America, such a utopian perspective could even present itself as a higher form of patriotism, since it was bolstered by the ideals expressed in the Declaration of Independence and the Constitution that had not yet been fulfilled. Moreover, the very idea of the Puritans who first arrived on these shores that they would build "a city on a hill" gave sanction and warrant to the utopian temptation and injected it into the American bloodstream.

Yet while all this might be true in the realm of theory, it was still logically and psychologically inherent in utopianism for its dissatisfaction with the real world to sour into bitterness and then to degenerate further into a self-righteous hatred when that world offered resistance to the schemes and dreams of the utopians for transforming it into the Kingdom of God on earth. A similar bitterness and hatred also ineluctably extended to the people who, in their ignorance and perversity and selfishness, refused to submit voluntarily to these same schemes and dreams. Such people were wicked and deserved no consideration. Hence, wherever the utopians were able to gain power, these wicked people were simply murdered as obstacles to the implementation of the new scheme and the realization of the great dream. This is what happened in Russia, and then China, and then Cambodia, where the Communists, for all their pretensions to being "scientific," turned out to be afflicted by the very disease that Marx himself had identified exclusively with the utopian socialists and that Lenin dismissed as "infantile."

I believed that there were protections in America against a seizure of power by utopians. Yet I did not—and do not—doubt that in the almost unthinkable event that such a thing might happen, it would culminate in the same murderous result. St. Augustine once said that the virtue of children resides not in their wills but in the weakness of their limbs; and I thought this was equally true of the utopians in America. The harm they were able to do, though bad enough, was kept within bounds by the relative paucity of their numbers in a country where good sense generally prevailed among the populace, and which was fortified by a political system where sheer numbers counted for more than they did in non-democratic regimes.

This sharpened my realization that, as there was a logic built into utopianism, so there was an obverse logic built into the acknowledgment of it as the source of the disease which I had contracted and had then helped pass on to others. It was that the institutional structure of American democracy—American democracy as it presently existed in the real world—provided a barrier against the terrible evils that could issue from even the most apparently benevolent utopian intentions. This institutional structure therefore must be defended against the people both at home and abroad who thought that it was bad, and an untiring effort must be made to open the minds of those who did not appreciate its infinitely precious value or the enormous achievement it embodied and represented.

More than merely being defended, it deserved exactly what Irving Howe had deplored: namely, to be "celebrated." It deserved this not alone in itself and because of the blessings of freedom and equal opportunity it bestowed on the Americans who lived under it, but also for the willingness it had shown to make huge sacrifices in going to war against the two main challenges that had been thrown up against those blessings in the twentieth century. After all, it was this much maligned "bourgeois" democracy, with its putatively squalid "middle-class values," that had first taken on the totalitarian threat from the Right in the shape of Nazism (itself a product of a utopian vision which, for once, did not wear a smiling face); and it was this same society that had armed itself with nuclear weapons, kept troops stationed in Europe, and twice gone to war, once in Korea and once in Vietnam—all in order to hold the line against the masked and hence more insidious totalitarian threat from the Left in the form of Communism.

As the significance of these facts sank in, I proceeded to act upon them both as a writer and as an editor. But in breaking ranks with the anti-American radicalism of the 1960s and becoming one of its most aggressive critics, I was not yet ready to drop the other shoe and join forces with the Right. For a brief spell I found a resting place among the Social Democrats with whom I had already been allied in the fight against the New Left on domestic issues. Most of them had supported the American intervention in Vietnam, and on this we differed. But the anti-Communist position on which their support of the war was based—and to which I had been committed in the 1950s before my conversion to radicalism—was now being reignited along with, and as part of, my refound love of America.

This alone was enough to keep me from becoming a Republican. I voted for Richard Nixon in 1972—my first Republican vote ever—because he seemed to me the lesser of two evils as compared with his Democratic opponent Senator George McGovern. I knew that in McGovern, with his campaign slogan "Come Home, America" (and with his history of having supported the Communist-controlled presidential candidacy of Henry Wallace in 1948, along with the Communist parents of all the "red-diaper babies"* of the 1960s), the radicals had found a mainstream political leader who was, down deep, one of their own. (Eugene McCarthy, their candidate in 1968, had most emphatically not been

---

*This brilliant phrase came not from their enemies but from the New Left sociologist Richard Flacks.

one of their own: in his heart, McCarthy knew they were wrong.) But I was still against the policy of détente being pursued by the Nixon administration (the enthusiastic backing of which by the business community slowed down the progress I had been making toward a fuller appreciation of capitalism). With the Soviet Union just then embarking on a great arms buildup, I thought that we should be devoting ourselves to preventing them from achieving military superiority. Instead, through the economic rewards that formed one component of détente, we were trying in effect to bribe them out of their ambition to "Finlandize" Western Europe and ultimately even the United States.

The leading exponent in American politics of the point of view I now held was Senator Henry M. Jackson. Unfortunately, however, an unsuccessful run in the Democratic presidential primaries of 1976, won by the impossible Jimmy Carter, made it clear that Jackson was not a viable candidate for the highest national office. (It was said that he was such a dull speaker that if he were to give a Roosevelt-type fireside chat, the fire would go out.) My hopes, and those of many who had emerged from the wars of the 1960s with ideas similar to mine, now came to rest on my old friend and veteran contributor to *Commentary*, Daniel Patrick Moynihan, who was elected to the United States Senate from New York in the same year Carter defeated Nixon's successor Gerald Ford in the race for the White House.

Moynihan ran as a Democrat, which is what he had been all his life. Even so, he had accepted an offer in 1968 by the newly elected Richard Nixon to serve in the White House first as a special adviser on domestic affairs, and then as ambassador to India. When Ford took over after Watergate had driven Nixon from office, Moynihan returned home from India and shortly thereafter he wrote a long article for *Commentary* entitled "The United States in Opposition." In this article, Moynihan deplored the acquiescence of American diplomats, particularly at the United Nations, in the continual assaults on the United States by the representatives of third-world despotisms. He argued that the time had come for us to stand up for ourselves against such abuse and to begin speaking proudly and loudly for the party of which we were the world's leader—the "party of liberty."

When this article appeared in the magazine, it created a sensation, and it also persuaded Ford and Henry Kissinger, who had stayed on as Secretary of State after Nixon's departure, that Moynihan should be asked to put his theory into practice as the American ambassador to the UN. Doing so, perhaps, more aggressively than they had bargained for, Moynihan went on for eight stormy months, delivering speech after speech extolling the virtues of democracy and excoriating the totalitarians and their sympathizers who dominated the General Assembly. Nothing like so sustained, and sophisticated, a celebration of America had been heard for years, and it elicited a wildly enthusiastic response. When Moynihan walked into a restaurant, the diners would all rise and applaud, and New York taxi drivers would screech to a halt to yell their approval of him. Accompanying him on such occasions, I realized that the long era of self-flagellation and self-hatred through which we had lived since the mid-1960s was finally reaching its end.

Another sign of the new climate was the fervency of patriotic sentiment let loose by the celebration on July 4, 1976, of the country's two-hundredth birthday. Even in liberal New York City, where the highlight of that celebration was an armada of "tall ships" magnificently gliding under sail into the harbor, huge crowds cheered and many wept. As I watched this spectacle and listened to the response it evoked, it seemed to me that I was witnessing a Freudian "return of the repressed" that was all the more explosive for having been kept down for so long.

It was this new explosion of patriotism that convinced me, among others, that Moynihan could win if he ran for the Senate. Nor would it hurt, in a state where the Jewish vote mattered so much, that he had led the attack at the UN on the infamous resolution passed by the General Assembly declaring Zionism a form of racism. And so—with a little help from me behind the scenes—Moynihan first defeated the leftist Bella Abzug in the primary and then the incumbent conservative Republican James L. Buckley in the general election, and became a U.S. senator.

Meanwhile, I myself was writing and publishing articles month after month that, on the one side, made the case for a more vigorous American response to the Soviet threat and, on the other, tried to explain to a generation whose memory had gone dim what it was that was being threatened and why we had a sacred duty to do everything in our power to defend and uphold and—again—celebrate it. Around this time, too, I fulfilled a longstanding desire to drive across the country, and when I did, I finally found out what "amber waves of grain" and "purple mountain majesties" were. The Rockies and the great national parks of the West—not to mention the Grand Canyon—were beyond anything I had imagined, and I felt that they supplied a living connection between this relatively young nation and the most ancient stages of creation itself.

But what got to me even more were the far less beautiful "amber waves of grain." Driving through that endless sea of food, most of it produced by the allegedly villainous "agribusiness"—that is, a very small number of people—I could only marvel at the immense richness of the American soil and the endless ingenuity of those who cultivated it, and I could only laugh derisively at the idea prevalent among my fellow intellectuals that America was a nation in decline. I laughed just as loudly everywhere I went, because everywhere I went—big cities and small towns—what I saw as I watched people going about their business was not listlessness but energy, not depression but high spirits, not decadence but health, not despair but faith in the future: their own and the country's too, a country they loved with a love that was very little different either in kind or degree from my own recovered and rekindled passion.

PART

IV

Dayyenu American-Style

In the end, I suppose, it all comes down to gratitude. Gratitude was once regarded as a great virtue. It is, for example, at the very center of Judaism, which requires the observant Jew to thank God so often that it is a wonder he has time for anything else. He pronounces his thanks upon seeing the sun rise and upon seeing it set; he gives thanks for every morsel he puts into his mouth, with a different blessing for each food after its own kind; and practically anything that happens to him (including bad things), or that he notices, calls for yet another acknowledgment of having been blessed. This is how it is, though perhaps less obsessively, with Christians as well. But in the last four decades or so of the twentieth century, gratitude went out of fashion. More than that, it was positively stigmatized as a form of complacency. Now its opposite, constant complaining, which had formerly been regarded as unseemly,* took its place as a virtue. Competitions even arose among different groups of Americans as to which had the greatest cause for feeling bitter, and rewards in the form of "compassion" and government subsidies were doled out to the winners.

Nor was it only ethnic, racial, or sexual groups who got into this unlovely act. Individuals did too. To experience and express gratitude to God for one's blessings might be a religious obligation for

---

*Even among blacks. As the novelist Ralph Ellison instructed all of us—including those of his fellow blacks who were spitting upon or had forgotten it—his people were the legatees of "a tradition which abhors as obscene any trading on one's anguish for gain and sympathy."

an observant Jew or a pious Christian, but under the new secular dispensation, dissatisfaction with one's lot became the mandatory spiritual state and obstreperous whining to the government the prescribed form of prayer. If, by the standards of this perverse pietism, one was sinful enough to be happy, especially if one was rich, or successful in some other way, the sinner was at least expected to have the decency to shut up about it and (in the words of the Second Book of Samuel in the Bible) to "Tell it not in Gath, publish it not in the streets of Ashkelon."

There were rare exceptions, mainly among businessmen like Donald Trump and Lee Iacocca, who seemed oblivious to this prohibition, and would probably have failed to understand its cultural power even if they had been aware of it. But the rich and the successful—even those who were genuinely grateful for what they possessed—had on the whole been intimidated enough to remain silent, lest they be mocked as doltish braggarts, or even get themselves investigated by the Justice Department.

Once in a great while, however, someone came along who understood the new ethos full well and set out deliberately to defy it. At which point the response—like the actor of whom a critic once said that his emotional range extended all the way from A to B— was likely to travel the distance from moral condemnation to political outrage. The most salient instance of such a response in many years was occasioned by the appearance in 1983 of a book by William F. Buckley, Jr. entitled *Overdrive: A Personal Documentary*.

The ugly hostility with which this exquisitely written, always witty, and utterly fascinating book was received might have been ascribed to the author's conservative political views, which were much in evidence. Yet by 1983, Buckley, through his ubiquitousness as a writer and television personality, and through a distinct mellowing of his fearsome youthful personality, had begun turning into a venerable presence on the American scene, in danger almost even of becoming a beloved one. At the same time the conservatism he had done so much to revive from the mid-1950s onward had also become much more acceptable than it was at the beginning.

To liberals in 1956, when Buckley founded *National Review*, the very idea of a conservative intellectual seemed a contradiction in terms: had not Lionel Trilling only recently established it as a truth universally acknowledged that there was no conservative thought in America?

Trilling's sweeping dismissal came in the preface to his book *The Liberal Imagination*, where he called it a "plain fact" that there were no "conservative or reactionary ideas in circulation" in "the United States at this time" (1950). No doubt, he acknowledged, there were strong impulses "to conservatism or to reaction," but these impulses did not, "with some isolated and some ecclesiastical exceptions, express themselves in ideas but only in actions or in irritable mental gestures which seek to resemble ideas." This assessment met with very wide acceptance and continued for a long time to be cited as authoritative (by me, among countless others). Yet the reason liberal ideas enjoyed the monopoly Trilling correctly attributed to them was not that there were no conservative intellectuals in America. It was, rather, that the ones who existed were treated as invisible, even by a heterodox liberal like Trilling, despite the fact that he himself had always been strongly attracted to their counterparts in Europe. In this very preface, Trilling deplored the debilitating effect on American liberalism of the absence of a strong conservative challenge to its increasingly complacent assumptions. But all he had to do was glance around at his fellow men of letters to spot such distinguished conservatives as Allen Tate and John Crowe Ransom—not to mention the master of them all, the expatriate T. S. Eliot. Glancing further afield, into other parts of the American intellectual forest, Trilling would also have come upon the likes of Leo Strauss, Ludwig von Mises,

Richard Weaver, James Burnham, and Peter Viereck, all of whom were just then busy at their labors. And far from being, as Trilling charged, "bankrupt of ideas," the conservative movement in America was already heavily pregnant with important books by Russell Kirk, Eric Voegelin, Will Herberg, Clinton Rossiter, Buckley himself, and others that would all be completed and published within the next few years. In ignoring or contemptuously dismissing the work of all these conservative intellectuals as self-evidently inferior and retrograde, Trilling, who in so many other respects (and in *The Liberal Imagination* itself) dissented from the attitudes of the liberal community, for once went along with the conventional liberal wisdom. Why he should have done so is a bit of a mystery.

Be that as it may, instead of allowing themselves to be killed off by being ignored or vilified or both, the conservatives had stayed alive, and by 1983 had even done much to put Ronald Reagan into the White House: Reagan, who was not only a close friend of Buckley's but who had often acknowledged a debt to the younger man for having helped him see the light by which he had been guided from liberalism to conservatism.

This alone would have been enough to override Buckley's growing acceptability and to get the vindictive juices of the largely liberal book-reviewing world flowing in a mighty regurgitative stream. Yet leafing through the reviews of *Overdrive* in preparation for writing one myself, I came to the conclusion that something deeper and more interesting than repugnance for Buckley's politics, or envy, or even resentment toward him for having helped Reagan become President, was at work in these vituperative attacks.

The book itself, cast in the form of a journal, was an account of a single, and presumably typical, week in Buckley's life. The frenetic nonstop activity of this man from early morning until late at night was vividly recorded, but Buckley, without the slightest trace of embarrassment, also zoomed in on the material circumstances in which he lived his life. The great luxuries of that life were dwelled upon lyrically and in almost lubricious detail: his big house on the water in Connecticut, which also contained "the most beautiful indoor pool this side of Pompeii"; the marvelous thirty-six-foot sloop that seemed "to ice-skate over the waves"; the outsize limousine driven by the perfect chauffeur (one of a host of equally perfect servants) that carried him from Connecticut to his house on East Seventy-third Street in New York, where the furnishings and the appointments would also have been at home in Pompeii; and so on.

Of his Connecticut home he wrote:

> My wife and I know what it is to learn to love a piece of property wholly; defiantly; truculently, even. . . . We'll always be here, then, in the warm summers when the leaves make invisible the houses of our neighbors to the south and north; in the spiky fall season, days like today with the little chill that makes one feel freshly laundered; and in the truly cold of the cold days. . . .

Thus the country. But the city was equally delightful in its very different way:

> I have read the newspapers and breakfasted in the beautiful, cloistered, red-red library Pat has so ingeniously decorated and then, in my dressing gown, I climb up the stairs to my little study, which incidentally looks out, between 8 and 8:30, on the handsomest, gayest, most cheerful parade of children aged six to twelve, the youngest of them accompanied by nurses or governesses, all of them carrying sackfuls of books, bouncing off to the multifarious schools concentrated in the area.

Equally delightful to Buckley was the social activity that filled his evenings and which he described in similarly effusive and glowing terms. So it went, then, hour after hour, day after day, from early morning until late at night, with this "blasphemously happy" man who was in love with the life he led. Buckley concluded with the following reflection:

> . . . if there were nothing to complain about, there would be no post-Adamite mankind. But complaint is profanation in the absence of gratitude. There is much to complain about in America, but that awful keening noise one unhappily gets so used to makes no way for the bells, and these have rung for America, are still ringing for America, and for this we are *obliged* to be grateful. To be otherwise is wrong reason, and a poetical invitation to true national tribulation. I must remember to pray more often, because providence has given us the means to make the struggle, and in this respect we are singularly blessed in this country. . . .

It was not surprising, not in the least, that those who both made and applauded "that awful keening noise" should have been moved instead to curses, contumely, and scorn. But to my mind, the only proper response to such a passage was a fervent Amen, which I pronounced then and have kept on repeating with even greater fervency ever since. Thanks to this habit of giving thanks, my spiritual and intellectual immune system was stronger than ever just when I would most need it. For, to my surprise, about fifteen years after the publication of Buckley's book, the anti-Americanism that, more than any other single element, had driven me out of the Left suddenly made an appearance in Buckley's own movement, in whose precincts I had (after some hesitation caused by a reluctance to, as it were, go all the way) eventually found a new political home.

Well, as I suggested in beginning the story to whose conclusion I am now heading, I had no call to be so surprised by this surfacing of anti-Americanism on the Right. For I was well aware that, un-like their European counterparts, who were almost always identi-fied with nationalism, American conservatives were the heirs of a long tradition of hostility toward their own country. This tradition extended at least as far into the past as the post–Civil War period, with—again the name inevitably crops up—Henry Adams as its most eminent spokesman. This was the same Henry Adams who was capable of writing the wondrous defense I quoted above of early America against its European critics without ever realizing that his own attack on the America of the Gilded Age echoed those critics in almost every detail, and that every one of the words he directed at them applied equally well to him.

In his youth, Adams entertained dreams of following his great-grandfather John Adams and his grandfather John Quincy Adams into the White House some day. But he was one of those people who lacked, both for better and for worse, the qualities it took—and still takes—to pursue a political career in a democratic society. Like Shakespeare's Coriolanus, he was too proud, too vain, and too arrogant to submit himself to the judgment of what John Adams had once contemptuously referred to as "King Demos." Instead of accepting this or blaming himself, however, Henry Adams blamed America, or at least what had happened to America as it became more and more industrialized, and more and more subject to the will and the appetites of King Demos, in the Gilded Age.

Having been a noble republic governed by distinguished figures like his own ancestors, America in Henry Adams's characteristi-cally bilious view had been stolen by a whole new class of business-men ("robber barons," as they later came to be stigmatized by other writers). Under these usurpers, America had degenerated into a country that worshiped only money and despised the higher things of life. To exacerbate the situation, in the wake of this new philistinism came the birth of a new political order, dominated by the corrupt machines of big cities like New York, Boston, and Chicago. These cities had themselves been ruined by the influx of immigrants on whom the new breed of political bosses depended for their power, and whose votes they could buy with the same ease with which they in their turn were being bought by the plutocratic likes of John D. Rockefeller and Jay Gould.

A completely different assessment of the "robber barons" and what they wrought would come more than a century later from two historians on opposite sides of the Atlantic and with differing points of view. One of them, Walter A. McDougall of the University of Pennsylvania, would explain in *Orbis*, the journal he was then editing, how he had arrived at this new understanding:

> During my research for *Let the Sea Make a Noise: A History of the North Pacific from Magellan to MacArthur*, I was struck by how differently the story of the . . . transcontinental railway is told . . . today than when I was a child. Back then, it was a triumph of the American spirit and nation-building, and the roles played by an enlightened federal government, visionary businessmen, and doughty immigrant labor—Irish and Chinese especially—were extolled.
>
> Today, the major theme of the story is always corruption, with the "Big Four" promoters of the Central Pacific . . . portrayed as robber barons who manipulated Congress, stock-jobbed on Wall Street, monopolized contracts and profits . . ., and generally swindled the public.

But, McDougall would go on,

> so great were the magnitude of what they achieved, the risks they took, and the energy and determination they displayed that I was moved to suggest that theirs was a "creative corruption," and that perhaps such creative corruption is a characteristic trait of great nations.

The British historian Paul Johnson, distilling in *Commentary* the conclusion he had reached on the same subject in writing his *A History of the American People* (1997), would go even further. He would credit "this collection of entrepreneurial individualists, united only by their colossal energy, native shrewdness, and belief in their country's future" with having "transformed a predominantly agricultural society into an industrial and financial superstate. . . ." If "we exclude the horrific gash of the still-inexplicable Great Depression," the century that followed the work done by these men, Johnson would point out, "has been mostly a saga of wealth-creation and wealth-distribution unique in world history . . . ," bringing to "the American people . . . an affluence never dreamed-of before. So whom did the barons rob?"*

An excellent question, if you ask me, but nothing approaching it ever violated the fine mind of Henry Adams, which could produce not so much as a smidgeon of approbation for the country America had become under the domination of the *arriviste* business class and its even more *arriviste* and corrupt political lackeys.† In

---

*There is also the usually overlooked fact that, as one of Rockefeller's biographers, Ron Chernow, would observe: "Our harshest industrial overlords proved our most enlightened philanthropists." To which it may be added that the money they gave away, mostly through building libraries, universities, and research institutes, did not lighten their tax burdens, since in those far-off days no such burdens existed.

†Since Adams took Edward Gibbon as one of his models, he might have been expected to have been familiar with the confident singling out by his great eighteenth-century British predecessor of corruption "as the most infallible symptom of constitutional liberty." (McDougall's gloss on this passing remark from *The Decline and Fall of the Roman Empire* was that "Given human nature, the more freedom a society enjoys, the more mischief it will engender.") But on the certain assumption that Adams knew the passage in question, he either disagreed with Gibbon or chose to ignore it. More seriously, and closer to home, he also chose to ignore that (in McDougall's words) "James Madison and the Founding Fathers took for granted the corruption of government by business, and business by government, and tried to design a federal system of checks and balances so that corruption could be contained and even work to preserve rather than efface American

such a country there was no place for a high-born and learned intellectual of his own caliber—or so Adams himself decided. That this was a self-serving assessment was recognized even then by some of his own friends. When one of them, the novelist Owen Wister (author of *The Virginian* with its legendary line, "When you call me that, *smile*"), asked what the matter was with Henry Adams, another friend, Oliver Wendell Holmes, replied that he "wanted it handed to him on a silver platter."

Nonetheless, Adams's transfer of blame for the frustration of his political ambitions from his own character to the character of the America into which he was unlucky enough to have been born was taken completely at face value by succeeding generations of writers and commentators, especially those who themselves derived from the old American patriciate. One such was Edmund Wilson. In speaking of his father's generation, which was roughly contemporaneous with Adams's, Wilson wrote:

> The period after the Civil War—both banal in a bourgeois way and fantastic with gigantic fortunes—was a difficult one for Americans brought up in the old tradition. . . . They had been educated at Exeter and Andover and at eighteenth-century Princeton, and had afterwards been trained, like their fathers, for what had once been called the learned professions; but they had then had to deal with a world in which this kind of education and the kind of ideals it served no longer really counted for much.

As it happened, Wilson disliked Henry Adams (he was one of the few dissenters from the judgment of Adams's autobiography,

---

liberties." This was precisely what would happen in the twentieth century in the form of a host of regulations that many would come to think had gone so far that a new set of checks and balances should be called into play from the other direction.

The Education of Henry Adams, as a great work—and so am I). This did not, however, prevent him from citing the dashed political hopes of Adams as a strong count in his indictment of the America that had emerged from the Civil War.

Another prominent literary critic, R. P. Blackmur, who unlike his contemporary Wilson was an admirer of Adams, found even less reason to question their view of the matter. As Blackmur saw it, Adams's "failure in American political society" had nothing whatsoever to do with any failings of his own. The fault lay entirely with "society's inability to make use of him: its inability to furnish a free field for intelligent political action." Once upon a time, Blackmur contended, there had been such a field, but America was now "bound for quick success. . . . It cared nothing for political mastery, and commonly refused to admit it had a purpose beyond the aggregation of force in the form of wealth."

Yet Wilson and Blackmur—together with the hordes of historians and intellectuals, preponderantly on the Left but on the Right as well, who churned out copy after copy of the same picture of America in the Gilded Age—simply ignored the abundant evidence that exposed the conception behind this picture as a myth, or at best as a very partial truth. What this evidence showed was that other young men with the same background and education that supposedly rendered Adams unfit for a political career in the new America were nevertheless able to enter public life and make a great mark on the times.

In the world of electoral politics, there was, for one, Henry Cabot Lodge. The scion of a family almost as eminent as the Adamses, a former student of Henry Adams himself when the latter taught at Harvard, a noted author, and a person of great intellectual gifts, Lodge became perhaps the most important United States senator of the age. Even more damaging to the myth, there was Theodore Roosevelt. Like Adams, Roosevelt was both a patrician and a historian (not so formidable or profound a writer or scholar as Adams but still the author of the four-volume work *The Winning of the West*, among other books). For all that, he wound up exactly in the position that, in the Adams-Wilson-Blackmur conception of the Gilded Age, he should by definition have been disqualified from reaching—the presidency of the United States.

If Lodge and Roosevelt succeeded in wooing King Demos, there were also among "the men in the clubs of social pretension, and the men of cultivated taste and easy life" (as Roosevelt described the members of his own class) a goodly number who managed to get themselves appointed to high positions and pursue great careers in public life. Oliver Wendell Holmes (like Lodge, an old colleague of Adams from Harvard) wound up as a Supreme Court justice, while Adams's closest personal friend John Hay was able to become Secretary of State.

For that matter, even Edmund Wilson's own father, who "had in his youth aimed at public life" but "could not be induced to take part in the kind of political life that he knew at the end of the century," served as attorney-general of New Jersey in the administration of Governor Woodrow Wilson (no relation).

Jumping ahead several decades to a more recent explosion of the anti-Americanism on the Right of which Adams was the most talented progenitor, we come upon the "Southern Agrarians" of the 1930s. This was a group of self-styled "reactionaries" mainly composed of literary people who were so full of disgust with the country emerging from the Civil War that they could make common cause with the Marxist literary intellectuals up north (including Edmund Wilson at that stage of his political evolution).

The Southern Agrarians were politically marginal even on their own home ground. They were also almost comically irrelevant in their opposition to industrialism and all its works, not to mention the nostalgia they felt for the antebellum South, which (slavery notwithstanding) they regarded as a far superior civilization to the one that had wiped it out in the Civil War. Even so, some members of this group, among them John Crowe Ransom and Allen Tate, went on to do important work as poets, literary critics, and editors. The "paleoconservatives," their intellectual and political descendants of the latter part of the century, were a lesser breed and could boast no adherent of even remotely comparable stature.

Yet just as a mutual contempt for capitalism had enabled the Southern Agrarians to join forces with Marxists who on most other issues inhabited the opposite end of the political spectrum, so the paleos themselves were drawn to a leftist *littérateur* like Gore Vidal. Here, though, the tie that bound was not so much animosity toward the crass "bourgeois" society into which—as the Southern Agrarians and the Marxists agreed from their respective vantage points a half-century earlier in the 1930s—America had hopelessly sunk. Certainly that sentiment remained alive and kicking in the 1980s and 1990s in an updated adaptation. But now it was mainly the nativism they shared that made Vidal acceptable to the paleos who, as strident nationalists of the Right, might otherwise have been expected to look upon so egregious a hater of America as an enemy.*

Here, too, in this invocation of nativism, an old right-wing tradition was being drawn upon and resurrected. This particular tradition had its origins in the "Know-Nothings" who arose in response to the arrival on American shores in 1848 of hordes of immigrants from Ireland. (There was also a sizable contingent of

---

*Whenever Vidal's vituperative assaults on America were described as anti-American, he would testily but also complacently retort that, on the contrary, he was the country's "biographer," citing as proof the series of potboiling novels he had written about past figures of American history ranging from Aaron Burr to Abraham Lincoln.

immigrants from Germany at the same time but, being mostly Protestant, they were considered less objectionable.) From that moment on, and until a halt was called in 1924, the number of 1848 Irish immigrants kept being multiplied by millions more of their own countrymen, and then their numbers were further swollen by still more millions of Italians from Sicily and Naples and Jews from Eastern Europe.

The Know-Nothing movement that came along to combat these "foreign" influences and to elect only native Americans to office was the vulgar expression of opposition to this enormously consequential phenomenon. But there was also a more sophisticated version. One of its leading exponents was the writer John Jay Chapman, another of Henry Adams's intellectual and social contemporaries (who, in Edmund Wilson's opinion, was a more pitiable victim of the Gilded Age than Adams himself). "A New York boy," said Chapman,

> who goes away to boarding school returns to a new world at each vacation. He finds perhaps on his return from boarding school, that the street where he and his companions used to play ball is given over to a migration of Teutons. When he returns from college, the Teutons have vanished and given place to Italians. When he reaches the Law school, behold, no more Italians—Polish Jews to the horizon's verge.

When he wrote these words, Chapman was not yet especially antagonistic to the foreigners who had been taking over his hometown. He did, however, believe that a homogeneous culture made for a higher level of civilization than the "kaleidoscope" New York had become.

So did even so large-minded and cosmopolitan a product of the American patriciate as the novelist Henry James. In 1905, after living abroad for thirty years, James returned for a visit, during which he was taken on a tour of the Lower East Side of Manhattan. There, sitting in the Café Royale, which was a gathering place of Yiddish-speaking writers and actors, he was impressed by their energy while at the same time worrying about the deleterious effect on the English language these people would ultimately have.

Such worries did not elicit any serious anti-Semitic reflections in James, as they would have done in Chapman. The worst James could manage was expressed through a slightly sinister question he asked himself: "Who can ever tell . . . in any conditions, . . . what the genius of Israel may, or may not, really be 'up to'?" But James's apprehensions over what the genius of Israel had in store for the future of the English language and its literature might have been dissipated altogether if he had been able to foresee how many of the children and grandchildren of these people whose cafés he had described as "torture-rooms of the living idiom" would be writing doctoral dissertations on, precisely, the novels of Henry James some fifty years later. In Chapman, by contrast, the tendency to glorify the virtues of an older America led in his last years to a virulent outburst of xenophobia directed against "the Jesuit and the Jew."

On this point, though no more an admirer of Henry Adams than his own champion Edmund Wilson was, Chapman joined hands with the man he had once sneeringly characterized as a member of "the Secret Society of the Only Intellectuals in America." For Henry Adams too developed into a vicious and obsessive anti-Semite. "The Jew," he wrote, "has got into the soul. I see him—or her—now everywhere, and wherever he—or she—goes, there must remain a taint in the blood forever." Or again: "I tell you Rome was a blessed garden of paradise beside the rotten, unsexed, swindling, lying Jews, represented by Pierpont Morgan and the gang who have been manipulating the country for the past few years."* Or yet again: "I am myself more than ever at odds with my time. I detest it and everything that belongs to it, with all its infernal Jewry."†

Gore Vidal fancied himself a member of the old American patriciate as exemplified by Adams and Chapman, and in one respect at least—his anti-Semitism—he was truly blood of their blood and flesh of their flesh. Prohibited by his leftism from directing his own nativist passions against the dark-skinned minority groups on whom the nativists of the last decades of the twentieth century largely focused, and seeming to have no interest in Catholics (the main bugaboo of traditional nativists, who feared that their loyalty to the Pope and the authoritarianism of their Church stood in the way of their developing into good Americans), Vidal conveniently made the Jews his principal target.

Curiously, however—as I mischievously but accurately told Vidal when we were still on speaking terms—his surname may well have pointed to a Jewish ancestry. That name (or variants like Vitale and Vitali), a translation of the Hebrew Chaim (meaning life), had always been very common among Sephardic Jews. Vidal was not pleased to hear this—and he refused to believe it even when I offered him the consoling compensation that a highly distinguished line had borne his name and that, even as a person of Jewish descent, he could still lay claim to the aristocratic status he so craved.

For all I know, my playful taunt may have contributed to forcing

---

*J.P. Morgan was not Jewish, and had no ancestral tie to the Jewish people, but it is unclear whether Adams thought he was or did, or whether he merely believed that Morgan was controlled by Jews. The latter interpretation seems more likely.

†If we subtract the anti-Semitism, we might think that Adams was an early incarnation of Edwin Arlington Robinson's Miniver Cheevy, that "child of scorn" who, because he had been "born too late," "grew lean as he assailed the seasons." When I was in my teens, as I have already mentioned, Robinson's poem about this character became one of my favorites.

Vidal's latent anti-Semitism to the surface, and yet not even he—famous for his breathtaking brazenness—dared in the post-Holocaust era to match Adams or Chapman in outspokenness on this issue. Therefore he had to disguise his anti-Semitism as "anti-Zionism." The same inhibition operated at the other end of the political spectrum in paleos like the commentator Patrick J. Buchanan (who took periodic vacations from his labors as a pundit to run for President on a nativist platform sufficiently sanitized to keep him from being placed entirely beyond the pale of respectable political debate).

Still, the disguise was so thin that the distinction between old-fashioned Jew-hatred and the newfangled anti-Zionism remained mostly invisible to the naked eye. Vidal and Buchanan might vociferously protest (borrowing a tactic from the apologists for the anti-Americans of the Left in the 1960s and adapting it to themselves) that all they were criticizing was the allegedly oppressive policies of the state of Israel toward the Palestinians.* But the main takers of this line were people who shared or were inclined toward their particular bigotries in the first place.

The paleos were centered at the Rockford Institute in Illinois, and had enough financial backing to publish two magazines. One was *Chronicles of Culture*, edited by one Thomas Fleming. The other was *This World*, edited by Richard J. Neuhaus, then a Lutheran pastor and later to become a Roman Catholic priest.

Neuhaus was not a paleo- but a *neo*conservative—that is, a former leftist who, like me, had broken with the radical movement of the 1960s, and out of much the same disgust with its anti-Americanism. It was therefore all but inevitable that he should have taken strong public issue with *Chronicles* for its nativism in general and its heaping of praise on Gore Vidal in particular. The upshot

---

*In their twisted view, dark-skinned peoples were fine so long as they did not live in America, and especially when they were fighting against Jews.

was a split by Rockford, which assumed the bizarre form of an actual raid staged in 1989 by emissaries from Illinois on the offices of *This World* in New York. Papers were confiscated, Neuhaus and his entire staff were physically ejected from the premises, and—lest they attempt to return—the office was padlocked.

Fortunately, several of the foundations that had been subsidizing this joint Illinois–New York publishing project sided with Neuhaus. He was thus able to reconstitute his operation under the name of the Institute for Religion and Public Life and to resume putting out his magazine, which (the title *This World* being owned by Rockford) was now rechristened *First Things*. Rockford and *Chronicles* were rewarded with a return to the marginal status that their point of view deserved, while in its new incarnation Neuhaus's journal became much more influential than it had been under its former auspices.

All the more amazing was it, then, when in 1996 *First Things*, of all magazines, published a symposium, "The End of Democracy?," which reminded me—and not me alone—of nothing so much as some of the attacks on America emanating from the Left in the 1960s. The grounds were different, and so were the motives, but for all that there were amazing similarities.

The most disturbing of these derived from the idea broached by several of the participants that the present American "regime" had become "illegitimate." The reasoning behind this charge was that the judiciary had grown so arrogant and had so overstepped its proper powers that it had subverted the system of checks and balances among the three branches of government which formed the very foundations of American democracy. The introduction to the symposium (written though not signed by Neuhaus) flatly declared that several recent decisions by federal courts were not only wrong in their interpretation of the Constitution but also morally indefensible. So indefensible, indeed, that persons of conscience now had to ask themselves whether the only proper responses were those "ranging from non-compliance to resistance to civil disobedience to morally justified revolution."

Outraged by such dangerous extremism, two members of Neuhaus's editorial board resigned in protest, and I myself (as a friend and a reader, not a board member) wrote him a very angry letter that began by saying that "I did not become a conservative in order to become a radical, let alone to support the preaching of revolution against this country." I then went on to upbraid him for resurrecting the worst aspects of the culture of the 1960s against which we had both rebelled:

> I am appalled by the language . . . you use to describe this country, especially your . . . reference to Nazi Germany; by the seditious measures you contemplate and all but advocate; and by the aid and comfort you for all practical purposes offer to the bomb throwers among us.

It was not the attack on judicial imperialism that bothered me. How could it, when for some twenty-five years, article after article in *Commentary* under my editorship had been railing against the same pathology, and when I had joined the chorus in my own writings as well? As recently as 1987, in the syndicated weekly column I was then doing, with the *New York Post* as my home base, I had even denounced the Supreme Court as "a lawless institution" for having twisted the Civil Rights Act of 1964 into a mandate for the very quotas and reverse discrimination expressly prohibited by Title VII of that act.

What had especially riled me up then was that this was not merely one of those instances of the Supreme Court's discovering things in the Constitution that ordinary mortals could not find there but that were supposedly implied by this or that clause. Troublesome as such cases were, they arguably fell within the scope of judicial review. In stipulating this, I was giving more due than I really believed it deserved to the notorious theory of "penumbras and emanations" that had been promulgated by Justice Harry Blackmun and that supposedly justified the Court in establishing constitutional sanction for rights that were never actually written into the Constitution itself. But I was thus bending over backward the better to show that the issue before us now was even more disturbing.

What made it so was that the Civil Rights Act of 1964, a law which, in undisputed accord with the Constitution, had in the plainest and most unambiguous language forbidden certain practices, was being converted by the Supreme Court into a law permitting, nay even requiring, *those* very practices. The language of the Act was plain as plain could be:

> It shall be an unlawful employment practice for an employer—(1) to fail or refuse to hire or to discharge any individual . . . because of such individual's race, color, religion, sex, or national origin; or (2) to limit, segregate, or classify his employees or applicants for employment in any way which would deprive . . . any individual of employment opportunities . . . because of such individual's race, color, religion, sex or national origin.

Equally unambiguous was the legislative history on which constitutional scholars also rely in determining the intent of the Congress in passing a given law. The floor manager of this bill in the Senate, the great liberal Hubert Humphrey, assured his colleagues that there was nothing in it that would "require hiring, firing, or promotion of employees in order to meet a racial 'quota' or achieve a racial balance." Humphrey even promised to eat the paper on which the bill was written if he should prove to have been wrong: a promise he never kept.

The court was thus now arrogating unto itself the power to perform acts of antinomian alchemy. But it most surely did not have any right to such a power—not under our system of government. I concluded by asking where we were to turn when it was the Supreme Court that subverted and perverted and violated the law and trampled so arrogantly upon our rights.

Analytically, this was as tough and as rough as any attack on the courts in the *First Things* symposium. Yet I did not follow through on it by declaring that even so egregious a usurpation by the judiciary of the constitutional function of the legislature rendered our entire system illegitimate. Nor did I advocate civil disobedience, and still less revolution.

On looking again today at the piece I wrote saying these things, I must admit that a reader might perhaps have been entitled to draw such an inflammatory inference from the analysis, especially as I did not explicitly disavow it. Still, this was not in any shape or form my intention. What I was trying to do was expose the problem in the starkest and most persuasive terms in the hope of helping to set into motion a restoration of the right balance among the branches of our government.

That such a restoration could be achieved had been demonstrated when one or another of the other two branches had similarly overstepped at various points in our history. To mention only the most recent examples, there had been cries during the Nixon administration against the "Imperial Presidency,"* and in passing the War Powers Act of 1973, Congress had engaged in a bit of imperialistic expansion of its own at the expense of the presidency.

---

*The phrase came from the historian Arthur Schlesinger, Jr. But it is worth remembering that, having spent most of his life arguing for the strongest possible presidency, Schlesinger had never detected anything "imperial" about his heroes Franklin D. Roosevelt and John F. Kennedy. When the hated Nixon became President, however, and laid claim to the prerogatives he had inherited from his Democratic predecessors, presidential power suddenly presented itself to Schlesinger and his fellow liberals as a threat to the Constitution. This was, by the way, long before Watergate.

Admittedly, it sometimes suited the political convenience of the White House or of Capitol Hill to palm off its responsibilities on the unelected Supreme Court. But there was at least a chance that if they were forced to confront the full implications of what they were doing when they did that, institutional pride and self-interest would trump political considerations. The other two branches would then, as each of them had done in the past, rise up and reclaim their own infringed-upon constitutionally mandated prerogatives.

If what provoked my own protest was the issue of reverse discrimination, what inflamed the *First Things* symposiasts was the much more radioactive question of abortion. Believing abortion to be murder, and having as a result of recent pronouncements by the federal courts given up a longstanding hope that *Roe v. Wade* (1973), the decision that had legalized abortion in the first place, would ever be repealed, these serious and devout Catholics and Protestants (among them Robert P. George, Charles Colson, and Neuhaus himself) who made up a majority of the symposiasts were now being faithful to the logic of their position.*

Yet I could see little difference between this position and that of the left-wing radicals of the 1960s who believed that the United States was both fighting an unconstitutional war in Vietnam and committing war crimes, up to and including genocide, along the way. Nor did the *First Things* symposium shrink from drawing the same conclusion the 1960s radicals had done in disavowing any obligation to obey what they were convinced was an illegitimate regime and in interpreting acts of violence against it as expressions of loyalty to a higher moral law. The theories of the anti-American

---

*Euthanasia, in the form of demands for the right to "assisted suicide," also came in here, but this was a much newer issue than abortion and not yet as solidly established.

Left had been used to defend the domestic terrorism engaged in by some of its most radical members (like the Weathermen). Now, in my appalled interpretation, the Right was for all practical purposes lending aid and comfort (not, to be sure, in so many words or through open declarations of approval, at least not in the *First Things* symposium itself) to the right-to-lifers who bombed abortion clinics or murdered doctors who worked in them.

Confronted with all this, I fell into a despair of my own over the possibility that I was now about to earn myself a new set of ex-friends on top of the ones I had made thirty years earlier in breaking with the Left. Fast approaching the age of seventy, I was too old to seek for yet another political home.

Fortunately, however, tempers (including mine) cooled after a while, especially when Neuhaus, in a lengthy response to critics of the symposium, backed away from the more extreme views of those of his contributors who had made explicit what he himself had mostly only hinted at.* But no sooner did this happen than the Clinton sexual scandals broke out. When, against all predictions on both sides of the political fence, the President's job-approval ratings kept rising instead of falling, another group of my conservative friends and allies went on the attack—this time not against the "regime" but against the American people.

This was an entirely new turn for the contemporary Right to take. In the more or less distant past, conservatives had been noted for their suspicion of and even contempt for the masses (John Adams's "King Demos" had encapsulated this attitude). But contemporary conservatives were very different in this respect. They had at a certain juncture become strongly populist, largely because they had reason to believe that the American people were on their side in the "culture war" they were waging on behalf of traditional

---

*He did not, I should point out, admit to backing away. Rather, he argued that the symposium had been misread by its many critics, who evidently had been afflicted with a loss of their normally acute powers of understanding.

values against the relativism and libertinism of the elite sectors of the society.

Once upon a time these elites had themselves been conservative—the American counterparts of European aristocrats. But in the latter part of the twentieth century they were overwhelmingly liberal. It was this transformation that had given rise to the new attitude among conservatives expressed most pungently by William F. Buckley, Jr.'s remark that he would rather be ruled by the first two thousand names in the Boston phone book than by the combined faculties of Harvard and MIT.

Yet now, all of a sudden as it seemed, the first two thousand names in the Boston phone book were failing to come through. Instead of condemning the philandering and the lying in which the President had been caught, popular sentiment as reflected in the polls was more outraged by Kenneth Starr, the Special Counsel who was prosecuting Bill Clinton for his crimes, than by Clinton himself for having committed them. Nor did a majority of the people see any good reason for the impeachment proceedings inaugurated by the House of Representatives, and they were by all accounts relieved when the Senate failed to convict.*

This was too much for another old friend of mine, William J. Bennett. A former occupant of cabinet posts and other high government offices, Bennett was perhaps the most articulate and eloquent spokesman for traditional moral standards in America.

---

*I must confess that I too was relieved. I had no doubt that Clinton was guilty of perjury and obstruction of justice, and neither did I doubt that he deserved to be removed from office. But to have kicked out a President with such high job-approval ratings would, I feared, have injected even more poison into the American political bloodstream than was already there. Even the forced resignation of Richard Nixon deepened the bitter divisions in the country, despite the fact that Nixon's ratings had dropped into the 20s by the time he left. Clinton's were in the 60s.

He had also been one of the strongest adherents of the view that the American people were as repelled as he was by the moral rot against which he had been inveighing in a series of best-selling books, in television interviews, and in speech after speech after speech. But now, even before Clinton beat the impeachment rap, Bennett confessed that he might have been wrong about the condition of the American people. What the case of Clinton proved, he reluctantly felt forced to admit, was that the rot had now moved beyond its usual confines in the Beltway and Hollywood and had leached into the country at large.

This was how he put it in extemporaneous remarks at a meeting of the Conservative Political Action Committee (CPAC):

> Here's one thing conservatives need to be clear about. We have been on a Washington-bashing spree for a few years now, talking about the moral vacuum in Washington. Let us now, clearly and unambiguously, state the unstated fear: the moral decline in Washington is not only in Washington, it is outside the Beltway, too. . . . Those opinion polls are . . . from all over the country. . . . That is an erosion. That is moral decline.

Bennett was not the only conservative to bemoan "the death of outrage," the term he used as the title of a book he went on to write. In that book, much to my relief, he downplayed his CPAC judgment of the general moral decline of the nation, and concentrated on making a powerful argument for the impeachment and conviction of Clinton. Then, a year or so later, he reinforced the relief his book had brought me. The occasion was a speech made by George W. Bush, during his campaign for the presidency, criticizing conservatives for placing so much stress on the country's cultural decline ("our gloom and doom scenarios"). Some of those thus criticized struck back, but Bennett defended Bush:

> I, for one, plead guilty to drawing attention to America's cul-

tural decline. In the early part of the decade, the task was to call attention to America's stunning social regression. . . . But today, the news is more encouraging. So, on an empirical level, Governor Bush is right. . . . The 1990s have seen remarkable progress on some key social indicators. . . . The task now is to advance the forces of social composition. And to those conservatives who are tempted to give way to pessimism, resignation, and even withdrawal, we must answer: no, it need not be so, and we will not allow it to happen.

In referring to the conservatives who were surrendering to pessimism and calling for withdrawal, Bennett was no doubt thinking mainly of the veteran activist Paul Weyrich, who had outdone even Bennett's CPAC speech in despair. Weyrich won this peculiar palm by advising conservatives, and particularly the serious Christians among them, to "secede" from the mainstream of American society and retreat into enclaves of their own which (so he apparently thought) could be quarantined against the pathologies of the surrounding culture.

In thus advocating the depoliticization of the Christian Right, Weyrich was trying to reverse a process he himself had done much to get going in the first place. This process had led to the formation by the Reverend Jerry Falwell of the Moral Majority in the 1970s, and had then been further developed and refined by Pat Robertson and Ralph Reed with the Christian Coalition. But, Weyrich was now saying, the effort had definitively proved itself a failure, and the time had therefore come for devout Christians to return to the old days when most of them had not been concerned with politics at all.

In those days of old—and I am now speaking in my own voice, not paraphrasing Weyrich—to the extent that Christians even bothered participating in political affairs, the lion's share of the evangelical Protestants among them, who lived in the South, had not been Republicans: they had been as "solid" for the Democrats as everyone else down there. But however they may have voted, politics was not a driving passion for them. Mainly they were content to "render unto Caesar what was Caesar's" and concentrate on the infinitely more important business of trying to save their own souls. This entailed going to church every Sunday, striving to live by the moral principles of Christianity, and raising their children to do the same. That they could see no conflict between such a course and their acquiescence or even participation in the oppressive treatment of the blacks in their midst was a case of the triumph of culture over religion; and in any event, the anomaly involved did not change the central theme of salvation through Christ around which their lives were built and their communities constituted.

Contrary to what liberals imagined, what pushed these people into becoming politically active was not the sudden birth of an aggressive desire to impose their beliefs on everyone else. No doubt few of them would have found anything wrong with helping to save the souls of those who had not yet seen the light, but this was not what they were trying to accomplish. Nor (with an occasionally exuberant but lonely exception which liberals did their best to cast as the rule) did they entertain any dreams of imminently reshaping the whole country in their own image or officially "Christianizing" it. What pushed them into the political arena was just the opposite impulse: it was the felt need to defend themselves against the aggressive desire of the *liberal* world to impose its beliefs on *them*.

Due to the actions of liberal organizations like the ACLU, and the courts that consistently seemed to enforce their interpretation of the two clauses of the First Amendment, traditionalist communities (and not just Christian ones) were caught in a pincer movement. On the one side, they were prevented in the name of the free-speech clause from protecting themselves and their children against the flood of books, movies, and television programs that showed, and—subtly, or not so subtly—endorsed, a degree of sexual freedom that was offensive to Christians and other traditionalists and a threat to their way of life. On the other side, in the name of a less than self-evident reading of the "establishment" clause, the traditionalists were stopped cold from putting up a fair fight in Neuhaus's "public square."

To pick a notoriously symbolic example, the "establishment" clause of the First Amendment was interpreted as prohibiting the posting of the Ten Commandments on the wall of a schoolroom, while the "speech" clause was simultaneously invoked to prohibit the suppression of films instructing children in "safe sex" (including lessons in how to masturbate, and how to use condoms in both vaginal and anal intercourse). On a slightly different but related topic, Irving Kristol said, in another of the quips for which he was justly renowned, that the current state of liberal thought amounted to this: a teenage girl had the right to perform sex acts on stage, so long as she did it for the minimum wage.

Having made my peace with Neuhaus, I worried that he might lend his support to this new attack on the American people, and that we might begin quarreling all over again. But, mercifully, again I was granted relief when he refused to participate in the conservative retreat from populism and the political action that went with it. In a long, complex, and beautifully nuanced interpretation of the response to the Clinton scandals, Neuhaus disagreed with the original assessment by Bennett, Weyrich, and others of what that response revealed about the American people. He also stuck to his guns against the strict "separationists" who held that the establishment clause of the First Amendment forbade the entry into the public square of attitudes and policies with an identifiably religious provenance. He intended, in other words, to eschew the path of secession and to go on fighting for the right of religion to make itself heard without apology in American political discourse.

I welcomed Neuhaus's stand, but my own take on this whole business was a bit closer to the one developed most fully by yet another old friend, Gertrude Himmelfarb, first in several articles and then, in 1999, in her book *One Nation, Two Cultures.* We diverged here and there, and differences of emphasis existed between her analysis and mine. But both of us, independently of each other, had borrowed and then updated and adapted the idea of the "two nations" from Benjamin Disraeli, who had applied it to the rich and the poor of Victorian England. Later, in the America of the 1930s, John Dos Passos (before moving, as he would eventually do, from Left to Right) also used the same phrase in the Disraelian sense in *U.S.A.* ("all right we are two nations"). But unlike Dos Passos or Disraeli before him, both Himmelfarb and I were referring to a moral and cultural divide (or an "ethics gap" in the terminology she borrowed from the pollster George Gallup) rather than an economic one. Our two nations, or cultures,* were defined not by money and the things money could buy; they were identified by moral beliefs and the radically different ways of life that such beliefs tended to generate and shape.

The taxonomy I preferred in distinguishing between the two nations (or cultures) was "liberationist" and "traditionalist." (Himmelfarb most often spoke of the "dominant"—that is, the liberal—as against the "dissident" culture of the traditionalists, which she also described as a "counter-counterculture.") But again like Himmelfarb, I thought that the war between them, which raged on just as fiercely as ever in the realm of rhetoric, was reaching a kind of *de facto* armistice on the ground. As she put it (after paying due attention to the moral degradation all around us):

> For the moment, let us be content with the knowledge that the two cultures are living together with some degree of tension and dissension but without civil strife or anarchy. Amer-

---

*In her book, she shifted from the "two nations" of her earlier articles to "two cultures," presumably in order to dispel the incorrect impression that the culture wars had literally torn the nation apart.

ica has a long tradition of tolerance which has seen it through far more divisive periods than the present, a tolerance that does not require, as is sometimes supposed, a diminution of convictions but that is entirely consistent with the strongest convictions. It is this kind of tolerance that serves as a mediating force between the two cultures, assuaging tempers and subduing passions, while respecting the very real, very important differences, between them.

Without disagreeing, I went somewhat further than she did here in seeing an as yet unspoken and unratified accommodation between the two sides. The traditionalists, that is, were being forced not merely into begrudgingly surrendering to but even accepting a wider zone of toleration, especially in matters of sex, than they would have preferred. Conversely, the liberationists were being pressured to give ground of their own, again largely in matters of sex, but also on issues like welfare and crime. Admittedly this was not always being done by either side with a good grace, but it was being done.

One could, as still another old friend of mine and of Himmelfarb's, Judge Robert H. Bork, did in 1996, in his book *Slouching Towards Gomorrah* (which George W. Bush would mention by name in his critique of conservative pessimism), look at the popular culture and see the complete rout of the traditionalists by the liberationists. Certainly there was more than enough evidence to back up Bork's gloomy reading, and he did a masterful job of marshalling much of it and bringing it together with blatant symptoms of decadence and degeneration in other areas of American life. But so far as the popular culture itself was concerned—and even before the unanticipated decline in the rates of crime and welfare during the last years of the millennium—my own reading was that under the surface, where Gomorrah seemed clearly triumphant, something very different was going on.

In this connection, I again thought of a dear old friend, the late

Huw Wheldon, who had once run the BBC Television Service. During a period when British television was very much less restricted than the American networks in what could be said and portrayed where sex was concerned, Wheldon would regularly issue a caution to the producers and writers he supervised. In line with contemporary fashion, he would tell them, they could—if they wanted to; and they did—get away with using obscene language and filming sexual encounters that approached the level of soft porn in explicitness. But they would simultaneously have to remember that "the deep mores of a people change very slowly" and that unless those mores were accorded respect under the surface, the dramatic shows being put on the air by these liberationist producers and writers would fail to attract or hold a sizable audience.

Wheldon was as right about America as he was about England. No doubt we were from one perspective "slouching towards Gomorrah," to use the image Bork adapted from Yeats, but we were also putting the brakes on our forward motion toward that apocalyptic destination. There were even portents that Yeats's "rough beast, its hour come round at last," might soon reverse course and begin moving, ever so slowly and with many detours along the way, if not exactly toward Bethlehem (as Yeats himself speculated, and some American Christians, with the new millennium in sight, hoped and prayed), then at least in a direction leading away from Gomorrah.

The political theorist and social critic Francis Fukuyama thought so too. In his book *The Great Disruption*, published in 1999, he speculated that the great dislocations of the 1960s and 1970s had just about run out of steam by century's end, and that signs were appearing of a reconstitution of the social order that had taken such a beating in those two decades. Fukuyama was seconded by the political scientist and moral philosopher James Q.

Wilson, who in reviewing *The Great Disruption* for *The Public Interest*, agreed that "some kind of 'renorming' of society" was, at least to some degree, in the works, with "ordinary people [about to] reclaim part of an older culture" and to "reassert a common morality." Fukuyama and Wilson accorded the necessary deference to the resistances, both cultural and institutional, that such a process would have to overcome and the rot that would still remain. But while each of them surrounded his optimistic forecasts with careful qualifications of his own, neither allowed the qualifications to cancel out the optimism.

The *de facto* armistice I saw developing all around me could also be defined in somewhat different terms. One alternative came from Neuhaus. In rebutting those who thought he had "let the American people off too lightly" in his reflections on the Clinton scandals, Neuhaus quoted the British writer G. K. Chesterton who in the 1920s had "visited America and declared it to be a nation with the soul of a church." But he then went on to quote the addendum by the British journalist Alistair Cooke that it was "also a nation with the soul of a whorehouse." Both generalizations, Neuhaus averred, were "amply supported by the evidence." (His conclusion was that "we have learned to hope with renewed intensity that Mr. Dooley was right when he said that God looks out for drunks, little children, and the United States of America.")

Yet another version of the shape of the armistice came from Mark Lilla of New York University in the *New York Review* in 1999:

> The 60s happened, Reagan happened, and for the foreseeable future they will together define our political horizon. As anyone who deals with young people today knows, Americans find no difficulty in reconciling the two in their daily lives. They see no contradiction in holding down day jobs in the unfettered global marketplace—the Reaganite dream, the

Left nightmare—and spending weekends immersed in a moral and cultural universe shaped by the 60s.

In 1999 as well, Jeremy Rabkin of Cornell, writing in *Policy Review* about "The Culture War That Isn't," offered his own not incompatible look at this entire subject:

> The truth about America seems to be far messier than a "culture war" between "orthodox" and "progressive" forces.* We are in the midst of many overlapping and cross-cutting social conflicts. Yes, there are deep divisions regarding public recognition or accommodation of religion and on social morals and "family values. . . ." But they don't at all line up neatly as cultural divisions between religious conservatives and secularizing "progressives."

To his own surprise, Rabkin's article drew down upon his head the wrath of several prominent conservatives who accused him of being blind to the horrors all around us. One of these, Thomas Sowell of the Hoover Institution, declared in a letter to *Policy Review*:

> All across this country, counter-cultural values are being relentlessly promoted in schools, libraries, museums, and even in corporations where "diversity consultants" harangue the employees with a counter-cultural interpretation of race and sex differences. We are not talking about mere differences of opinions or media biases or academic political correctness.

---

*This particular taxonomy, which defines the two contending armies in the culture war as the secularists and the religious (of any and all denominations), Rabkin borrowed from two very influential books by James Davison Hunter of the University of Virginia.

We are talking about very well-thought-out and systematic institutional efforts, including indoctrination that begins on campus with freshman orientation and includes whole departments of victimhood studies, coed bathrooms, and the portraying of pedophilia as just another lifestyle.

In defending himself, Rabkin acknowledged that American popular culture was more debased than in the past and that "doctrines of moral chaos" were being promulgated in various quarters. But he also insisted that "not all the current cultural trends are so discouraging," citing as evidence what he saw at his own university:

Compared with the bulk of students I observed here in the mid-1970s, today's students are far more likely to be involved in prayer or Bible study groups. They are far more respectful to fellow students in military uniform (as ROTC cadets). They display far more understanding and appreciation for the benefits of free markets. In a lot of ways, students are much more conservative than they used to be. I expect that, eventually, the faculty will improve, too.

In my own view, this was too sanguine, especially about the faculty, but undeniable as Sowell's indictment was, I could not help finding merit in Rabkin's counsel against conservative despair. Indeed, as the twentieth century approached its end—an event that would almost exactly coincide with my seventieth birthday—I had the impression, as a longtime warrior against the political leftism I embraced in my thirties and the liberationism in which it expressed itself culturally, and as a more recent soldier in the fight against the anti-Americanism of the Right, that some kind of peace was at hand.

Being neither a prophet nor the son of a prophet but a scribbler and a former fiddler with the scribblings of others, I was not about to make any predictions as to what lay in store for this country with which I was madly in love. There were those who were not so diffident, but I was highly skeptical or even downright incredulous about most of their forecasts—especially the claim that human nature itself was on the point of being altered by the microbiologists and the neuroscientists. Besides, having entered even by today's higher standards of longevity into old age, I found it, as the elderly always have, more comfortable (and less threatening!) to look back than to look ahead.

Before I conclude doing just that, I suppose I should make it clear that in telling the story of my love affair with America, and in trumpeting the gratitude that goes with it, I am not at the same time being uncharacteristically humble (a trait for which I have never been exactly famous). I am not, that is, suggesting that I was merely the passive recipient of arbitrary dispensations from the hand of a benevolent patron on high, or that I was the beneficiary of a policy of affirmative action *avant la lettre*. Not at all. I was born with certain gifts, I worked hard to cultivate and then to use them as fully as I had it within me to do, and in that way I earned the rewards they brought without special favors or allowances, and often even in defiance of those with the power to withhold or deprive me of those rewards.

Yet there are two senses in which the credit still belongs to America. One is the laws through which the American government, and the ethos of American society, encouraged private individuals (such as Joseph Pulitzer and Euretta J. Kellett) to set up scholarships and fellowships like those that enabled me to attend Columbia and Cambridge; then too the government directly funded grants of its own (through the Fulbright program) that helped prolong my stay in England while providing me with enough extra money to travel all over Europe. It was also the tax exemption extended by American law to nonprofit institutions that made *Commentary*—and hence much of my life's work—possible.

Finally, the same laws and the same philanthropic ethos that enabled me as a youth to attend Columbia and Cambridge are now, in my old age, helping me through generous foundation grants to keep going as a writer. But it is important to stress again that this philanthropic ethos was born (among those notorious "robber barons") long before there were any tax advantages in it.

There is also another, more important and deeper, sense in which America can be credited with so many of the good things that happened to me, and it lies at the very heart of the American Revolution. According to some theories, the American Revolution was not a revolution at all, but a civil war in which Englishmen who had been denied their rights as Englishmen seceded from the mother country. This was why Edmund Burke, who would become the most unyielding and eloquent critic of the French Revolution in 1789, had been a supporter of the American uprising against his own country in 1776. But I have often thought that the American Revolution, in addition to being successful in achieving its goals—which is more than can be said for the French, let alone the Russian, one—was also the most revolutionary of them all.

What made the American Revolution so revolutionary was that it set up a system in which, for the first time in human history, individuals were to be treated as individuals rather than on the basis of who their fathers were. I know, I know: this principle was trampled upon by the continued existence of slavery, and also mocked in such lesser matters as the denial of the franchise and of equal economic opportunity to women. But to the repeated frustration of the utopians, some of these breaches were inescapable, being caused by the nature of things itself which prevents any system from entirely doing away with the advantages of being born into a wealthy or talented family, or to eradicate the tendency toward social snobbery, or to succeed (as we tried to do in the latter part of the twentieth century) in pretending that there are no differences of any consequence between the sexes. Even so, from the moment this country was born, the principle was always honored *in principle*, and to a greater extent in practice than even some of the men who designed the system anticipated would be possible.

The means through which it was honored in practice were the creation within the system itself of conditions for, or the removal of obstacles to, the opportunity granted each individual—or the "common man," as he used to be called—to use whatever talents and energies he possessed in bettering his own lot. The assumption was that this not only constituted a good in itself, but that it would be the best way for the individual to better the lot of others, starting with his own family and the community immediately surrounding him. A two-hundred-year trial—punctuated by occasional setbacks and requiring a civil war, the bloodiest ever fought by Americans anywhere, to remove the great contradiction which had been allowed to stand as the price of bringing all the colonies into a single polity—has demonstrated that the assumption was correct.

It was correct for the nation as a whole, and it was also correct for me personally. Which is to say that what America has done for me could not have been done for me alone, and could not have been done at all if the institutions, ideas, and attitudes that grew out of its founding assumption had not been in place and applicable to all who were lucky enough to live under them.

The word "all" brings me back one last time to race—the other great issue of the 1960s, which played a part in the fight over domestic affairs analogous to the role Vietnam assumed in foreign policy. Just as the radicals used Vietnam to discredit the entire policy of containment of which it was a product and an extension, so they interpreted the riots in the urban ghettos as proof that the traditional American method of lifting initially poor minority groups into the middle class could never work for the blacks. And just as the radicals succeeded in selling their point of view on Vietnam to the liberal elites who had themselves designed the policy of containment and had in its name led the country into the war, so they caused a similar loss of faith, and a correlative failure of nerve, among those same elites in the system of assimilation or integration in which they had previously believed.

With respect to Vietnam, this created the unlovely spectacle of the erstwhile supporters of American policy rushing as fast as their aging legs could carry them to the head of the parades marching against it. Unlovelier still, it transformed many of them (like George F. Kennan, the father of containment; McGeorge Bundy, the hawkish National Security Adviser under Presidents Kennedy and Johnson; and Robert McNamara, the equally hawkish Secretary of Defense in the same administrations) from the anti-Communists they had been into anti-anti-Communists.

In this new incarnation, they would now devote themselves to fashioning schemes to "end the arms race" that were so one-sided as to amount to a call for the unilateral disarmament of the United States, not to mention other measures that betrayed the hope they had once entertained of some day seeing the Soviet empire crumble and Communism along with it. In 1947, Kennan thought that containment would bring this about in fifteen years. He was right that it would work, but way off on the timing: it actually took a little over forty years—taxing his own patience to the breaking point—and needed for its consummation the reinforcements provided by Ronald Reagan through an arms buildup and the threat of an American defense against missiles.

A similar turnaround occurred among liberals on race. Since the post–Civil War period, America had been a highly heterogeneous society, but—again with occasional exceptions—it had found a way to translate the slogan "*E pluribus unum*" engraved on every coin into a reality. It had done this, moreover, with a minimum of the violence and the repression that were invariably experienced by other countries made up of a variety of religious and ethnic groups. The way it found consisted of a mixture of elements: the treatment of individuals as individuals in accordance with their own merits and without reference to their ancestry, plus the provision of the type of free public education I received as the child of immigrants.

It was a system of which most Americans approved and were proud, and from which every minority group had benefited, except—or so it was widely believed—the blacks. This belief ultimately begat a loss of faith in the old way, and that in turn begat the concept of affirmative action. Yet even as the liberal elites were being convinced by the radicals that no progress had been or could ever be made by blacks under the system by which each individual was supposed to be treated as an individual without regard to "race, color, or creed," the evidence proved otherwise. Thomas Sowell, summarizing the conclusion of his own extensive research as well as that of Stephan Thernstrom of Harvard and Abigail Thernstrom of the Manhattan Institute in their richly documented book *America in Black and White* (1997), would put it bluntly after the new system of preferential treatment had been in place for about three decades: "[T]he rate of progress of blacks, and especially of low-income blacks, during the era of affirmative-action policies has been less than that under the 'equal opportunity' policies which preceded it, or even *before* equal opportunity policies." (The italics are mine.)

Though I vehemently opposed affirmative action from the first minute it made its appearance on the American scene around 1970, I must admit that I owe this policy a kind of debt, because having to build a strong case against it was one of the intellectual tasks that helped me understand better than ever before the principles on which America had been established and through which it had grown great. Thus, one of my main arguments was that this presumably liberal or progressive idea actually represented a reversion to a state of affairs under which the individual was once again to be looked upon as the member of a group or a class and dealt with on that basis alone: the very state of affairs that the American Revolution was fought to overturn. As such, affirmative action was both a part and a result of what Sowell would later strikingly describe as a campaign to effect "the quiet repeal of the American Revolution."

Another of my arguments concerned the accompanying notion of social justice as the distribution of rewards and benefits to these newly recognized groups in proportion to their relative size within the population as a whole. Here we had an idea that was wholly new to the distinctive American ethos, and another counterrevolutionary reaction against it. Aside from conflicting with the liberalism in which its proponents still professed belief, it was offensive to the American legal and constitutional order (not that the liberals on and off the courts could be brought to see or admit this). I did not hesitate to say further that this new conception of social justice, while granting preferential treatment to blacks, would also foster discrimination against Jews. Being less than 3 percent of the population but earning a much greater share of wealth and position, Jews would have to be cut down to size (not that many liberal Jews could be brought to see or admit *this*).

Two more points are worth making on the subject of Jews and affirmative action. The first is that most of them favored it, which was another proof that Jewish support for blacks was not based on self-interest (though, to repeat something else that cannot be stressed too often, there was something unhealthy and lacking in self-respect in this refusal to stand up for one's own). The second point is that my worst fears in 1970 about what affirmative action would do to Jews never materialized. It has been suggested, not altogether in jest, that the reason was that when women got into the preferential-treatment act, the Jews among them (seen not as Jews but as women) made up numerically for whatever disadvantages might have accrued to Jewish males.

At the dawn of a new millennium, signs are beginning to appear that, in spite of their entrenchment and the interests that will fight to the death to keep them alive, affirmative action and its close cousin bilingualism may be on the way out. They have caused a great deal of harm during their long run, not least to their intended beneficiaries whose achievements have been put under suspicion as having been granted rather than earned. But that they have not been even more damaging is a tribute to the strength and resiliency of this country and the political, economic, and social traditions by which it has been governed and guided (sometimes, as in recent years, without realizing it) for more than two centuries.

True, we still have a black "underclass" that has remained impervious to the system whose workings have brought so many blessings to everyone else. At the same time, it has remained equally resistant to the endless energies and the billions of dollars that the government has spent in trying to help it out of the morass in which generation after generation of its members have been stuck.* But in my judgment as a one-time enthusiast of such

---

*Depending upon how broadly it is defined, the underclass has been estimated to comprise anywhere from 2 to 10 percent of the black community. Stephan Thernstrom, who has probably made at least as thorough a study as anyone of the relevant factors and the statistics they yield, thinks that the 2 percent estimate is the most accurate. There are whites in the underclass as well, but their number is so small as to be statistically insignificant. As for the poor, who live on the next rung of the economic ladder (and more of whom in terms of absolute numbers, as opposed to percentages, are white than black), Sowell reports that only 3 percent remain in the bottom fifth of the income distribution for more than eight years. This alone distinguishes them from members of the underclass, one of whose prime characteristics is that they stay where they are from one generation to the next.

efforts, the underclass will never be saved until the *real* "root causes" of its existence are addressed.

These, as almost everyone now recognizes, are neither white racism nor a paucity of jobs but the cultural and moral conditions in which "babies have babies" and in which boys and young men are free to seduce one set of such babies and to sire the other without assuming any responsibility for either of them. The only thing left for government to do is stop providing incentives to the creation of such conditions, and it has begun at long last to do just that through various reforms of the welfare system. There may also be hope in the so-called "faith-based" projects that have been coming out of the churches and that are focused on precisely the right factors. Just how much hope can realistically be held out, however, is hard to gauge, the intractability of this problem being what it is.

But there I myself go, doing what I deplore in others by concentrating on the little that is wrong with America instead of the enormous good embodied within it. From our modern perspective, much more was wrong with Periclean Athens, or England under the first Queen Elizabeth and then under Queen Victoria, or Russia under the czars. But this did not prevent them from being among the very highest points of human civilization and achievement. I believe with all my heart that the United States of America belongs on that list. We have not earned a place on it, as the others mainly did, by our contribution to the arts. In this respect, we have not fulfilled the dream of John Adams:

I must study politics and war that my sons may have liberty to study mathematics and philosophy. My sons ought to study mathematics and philosophy, geography, natural history, naval architecture, navigation, commerce, and agriculture, in order to give their children a right to study painting, poetry, music, architecture, statuary, tapestry, and porcelain.

Yet as I have repeatedly tried to show, even in the sphere of the arts we have not done too badly. We have, in fact, done far better than might generally have been expected of a nation conceived primarily to achieve other ends. These (as the normally hard-headed Adams himself knew when not seized by an uncharacteristic lyrical fancy) were political, social, and economic, and it is in them that we have indeed excelled the most.

We have excelled by following our founding fathers, Adams included, in directing our energies "to the preservation of the blessings of liberty for ourselves and our posterity," as well as to "the pursuit of happiness," tacitly understood to require prosperity as a necessary precondition. (In his original draft of the Declaration of Independence, of course, Jefferson used the word "property" rather than the phrase "the pursuit of happiness.") By remaining, in spite of lapses like affirmative action, faithful on the whole to the methods by which the founding fathers hoped to accomplish these ends, we and our forebears have fashioned a country in which great abundances of liberty and prosperity are more widely distributed and shared than among any other people in the history of the human race.

So far as liberty is concerned, we all, "rich or poor, young or old," in the words of the old song "I Am An American," have so much of it that some of us think we have too much for our own good. But scarcely anyone except the libertarians complains about the lack of it. As for those who complain about the "growing gap" between rich and poor and similar economic woes, they either are tendentious in their use of statistics or are basing themselves on questionable assumptions about social justice and fairness.

These assumptions, moreover, are not only dubious in themselves but run against the American grain. What Tocqueville observed in the 1830s remains true today: Americans, unlike Europeans, "do not hate the higher classes of society" even if "they are not favorably inclined toward them. . . ." Which is to say that most Americans do not share the obsession of their self-appointed spokesmen of the Left with the issue of who gets how much, or the accompanying passion for economic egalitarianism that made for the spread of socialism in other countries. Surely it is the absence of that passion—deprived of nourishment, as it has been more often than not, by the opportunities to better one's own lot, and the advantage millions upon millions upon millions have been able to take of those opportunities—that explains why socialism never has had much appeal in the United States.

Another, related, reason for the unpopularity of socialism here is that even the poor among us—and even some of the poorest—enjoy material amenities and conveniences like indoor plumbing, cars, color television sets, washing machines, and so on that in large parts of the world are luxuries available only to the rich. As of the end of the twentieth century, the average middle-class family seemed rich by the standards both of the recent American past and the international present. Yet even more than 40 percent of Americans *defined as poor* (that is, with annual incomes of $13,200 or less for an average size family) owned their own homes, 72 percent had washing machines, 60 percent owned microwave ovens, 92 percent had color television sets, half had air conditioners, and 72 percent owned *one or more* cars.*

---

*This kind of thing has been true almost from the beginning. "The word poor is used here," wrote Tocqueville in a footnote of his own, ". . . in a relative, not an absolute sense. Poor men in America would often appear rich in comparison with the poor of Europe. . . ." Tocqueville further observed that in America "the poor, instead of forming the immense majority of the nation, as is always the case in aristocratic communities, are comparatively few in number, and the laws do not bind them together by the ties of irremediable and hereditary penury."

These astounding figures came from a book by W. Michael Cox of the Federal Reserve Bank of Dallas and Richard Alm of the *Dallas Morning News* entitled *Myths of Rich & Poor: Why We're Better Off Than We Think*, and were based on studies by the Federal Reserve Bank of Dallas itself. According to Cox and Alm, "by the standards of 1971, many . . . poor families [of 1998] might be considered members of the middle class." Cox and Alm also showed that, measured by consumption (to some extent, admittedly, increased with the help of government subsidies), the proportion of the poor in the United States had declined from 31 percent in 1949 to a mere 2 percent fifty years later.*

In an article in *Commentary* reporting on these findings, the economist Irwin Stelzer of the Hudson Institute went on to expose the fallacy of the argument that inequality was increasing in America because of "the premium the market place accord[ed] to [an] education . . . [that was] out of reach of many." He wrote:

As the rate of return on education has risen, so has the number of people of all income groups seeking such training. . . . In 1970 only 55 percent of men and women over the age of 23 had completed four years of high school; by 1998 that figure was well in excess of 83 percent. In 1970 only one-third of high-school graduates between the age of 18 and 24 enrolled in college; now, some 45 percent do. And the number is rising.

---

*Inevitably, some of the claims made by Cox and Alm, and some of their statistical methods, have provoked controversy and have aroused the ire of left-wing critics. But so far as I have been able to determine, while the Cox-Alm analyses of income distribution and wages have been disputed, no one has challenged the accuracy of their enumeration of what is owned by the poor in America. And to the undying chagrin of the Left, what most Americans care about is what *they* have, not what Bill Gates and George Soros have.

The point, then, stands: more Americans (including black Americans) enjoy more freedom and more prosperity than any other people on the face of the earth, whether in the past or in the present.

Surely this entitles the United States of America to a place among the very greatest of human societies. And even more surely, it entitles this country to the love and gratitude of all whom a benevolent providence has deposited on the shores of—yes, a thousand times yes—"the land of the free and the home of the brave" to live their lives and make their livings under the sublime beauty of its "spacious skies" and "from sea to shining sea."

It is in this spirit of love and gratitude that, looking back as a septuagenarian on my life as an American in America, I am again reminded of something Jewish—this time of a special hymn of thanksgiving. It is included in the *Haggadah*, the book that Jews read aloud while conducting the *seder*, the festive meal they are required to eat on the holiday of Passover. In this hymn are listed all the elements making up the great event commemorated by the holiday—the liberation of the ancient Hebrews from slavery and their deliverance to the Promised Land of Israel—and a few more for good measure. Each element is the subject of its own sentence, and each sentence of the series concludes with the word *dayyenu*, which can roughly be translated as "That alone would have been enough for us." The idea is that, not content with "that alone," God went on and on and on to pile up wonder after wonder and marvel after marvel: so many that those participating in the *seder* invariably grow fatigued by the time they finish reciting them all.

America is not God, but it declared its independence as a nation by an appeal to "the laws of Nature and Nature's God," and the Constitution its founders wrote and ratified for that new nation uses the word *"blessings"* in its very first paragraph. The particular blessings to which they referred were those of liberty, to "secure" which to themselves and their posterity they created the Constitution that set the United States of America on its course.

For this, we, who *are* their posterity, either by blood or by adoption, should be giving daily thanks. We should be giving thanks for the establishment of justice (defined by John Adams as "a government of laws, not of men"). We should be giving thanks for a "domestic tranquillity" that has more often than not been "insured." We should be giving thanks for the "common defense" that has kept our homeland safe for so long from foreign invasion or destruction from the skies. We should be giving thanks for the "general welfare" that has been "promoted" by all these other blessings beyond the dreams of ancient avarice.

Any one of these blessings would have been enough; but America gave us all of them together, one following from another, and weathering challenges great and small for the two long centuries since President George Washington issued a Proclamation in 1789 at the request of both houses of Congress "to recommend to the people of the United States a day of public thanksgiving and prayer, to be observed by acknowledging with grateful hearts the many and signal favors of Almighty God, especially by affording them an opportunity peaceably to establish a form of government for their safety and happiness." In honoring Congress's request, Washington went on to speak in his own words of "the great degree of tranquillity, union, and plenty" the nation had enjoyed since achieving its independence and "for the civil and religious liberty with which we are blessed, . . . and, in general, for all the great and various favors which He has been pleased to confer upon us."

Such is the *dayyenu* that applies to all Americans alike, and that ought to be drowning out the "awful keening noise" about which William Buckley expressed his eloquent distaste in 1983—the noise that kept, and still keeps, us from hearing the bells still ringing for America and for which "we are *obliged* to be grateful."

But this having largely been the story of my own love for and gratitude to America, I think it might be more appropriate to end it with an American-style *dayyenu* that applies to me personally:

- If America had only granted me the inheritance of the English language, that would have been enough. But . . .
- Not content with that, America then sent me to a great university, which my parents would have been unable to do on their own, and where I could learn how to enjoy the riches of my cultural inheritance as an American.
- Not content with that, America then provided me with three wonderful years at another great university across the sea and the opportunity to see the world while I was there.
- Not content with that, America offered me the chance to make a modest but decent enough living doing the kind of intellectual work I would happily have done for nothing.
- Not content with that, America opened the way for me to meet and mingle and live my life with some of the most interesting people of my time: people endowed with great intelligence and erudition, or with great power, or with great wealth—and sometimes all three.
- Not content with that, America handed me a magazine of my own to run when I had only just reached the age of thirty, and allowed me to go on running it with complete freedom and independence for thirty-five years even when I was spending ten of them ungratefully attacking almost everything about America itself.
- Not content with that, America saw to it that I would live in an apartment in Manhattan much like the one in which the affluent parents of some of my classmates at Columbia had lived.

• Not content with that, when I retired after thirty-five years as an editor to devote myself mainly to writing, America arranged for me to build a country house on the East End of Long Island which (I think) is at least as big and well appointed as the one I had wept in as a kid in Wisconsin.

• Not content with that, America ensured that I would be writing these very words in that very house behind an un-painted wooden door that, like every other door both here and in my New York apartment, snaps shut with the very same satisfying click that so mysteriously broke the dam of tears in the nineteen-year-old boy I was more than fifty years ago.

ENDNOTES

1. The Hebrew name he was given at birth was Yoel, or Joel in English. But for some reason, he chose, or more likely was told to choose, Julius, possibly because it seemed to have a more American ring in the ears of the older relatives with whom he stayed when he first arrived here in 1912 as a boy of sixteen. As for Podhoretz, it is Ukrainian and means under, or at the foot of, the hill. Variants of the same name exist in all the Slavic languages (Podgorny in Russian, for example) and equivalents can also be found in most other languages (Underhill in English, Unterberg in German, Piedmont in French, etc.). Like all these, "Podhoretz" may have been taken from a town in the foothills of a mountain range, probably in this case the Carpathians. Never having been told of this by my father or anyone else, I simply assumed, once I discovered that a village with a close approximation of that name existed in the Ukraine, that some unknown ancestor of mine had migrated westward to Galicia at some unknown point in time. But then I learned that there was a little town called Podgórze in Galicia itself from which this mysterious ancestor may have traveled only a short distance south, to Lopatin or Witkew, the two neighboring villages from which all the members of that side of my family who came to America originally hailed. Almost all bearers of the name Podhoretz, which many people have trouble pronouncing, changed it in America to Podhurst. But not my father and one of his cousins, who held on to it as a matter of pride. The correct pronunciation is Pod-hór-etz, with the accent on the second syllable and the "h" sounded, but the few male descendants of the

cousin who passed it on place it on the first syllable, making it sound like Póderetz. After much badgering by me, they finally acknowledged that they were mispronouncing their own name, but their justification was that they got tired of correcting everyone who, upon seeing it, almost always would pronounce it that way. As for me, I have given up correcting anyone and will settle for any reasonable approximation.

2. Her Hebrew name was Khana, but Henyeh—a Slavic variant imported into Yiddish—was what she was always called. Like my father, she could have used the English version of her true name— Hannah or Anna—but again as with Julius, Helen must have sounded more American. Of course—this time unlike the Joel-Julius of my father's case—Helen had no relation either to Hannah or Henyeh except for its first initial. Neither, for that matter, did my own name, which was Naphtali in Hebrew and became Norman in English, with which its only connection is the first consonant. This having been a fashionable name among Jews of that day, many a baby boy of my generation, while introduced to God (or, if one prefers, initiated into the Jewish people) at his circumcision as Nachman or Nachum or Natan, was registered as Norman on his birth certificate. One of these, seven years older than I, was Norman Mailer, né Nachum.

3. East European Jewish males almost always had intelligible Hebrew names, by which they were, among other things, summoned to pronounce blessings over a portion of the Torah reading on the Sabbath and other sacred occasions. The few interesting exceptions were names like Sender (from Alexander) and Feivel (from Phoebus, as, amazingly, in Phoebus Apollo), both of which had presumably come down from the Hellenistic age and were then Yiddishized. The women, by contrast, were often known from birth only by Slavic names, also assimilated into Yiddish, with the Hebrew originals (if there were any) sometimes buried so deep that one could never be sure what they might be. Such was the case with the name Runyeh, which could have been a corrup-

tion of the Hebrew Rina or perhaps even Rachel. My maternal grandmother, on the other hand, was Esther Malkah (Esther the Queen: a misnomer of gigantic dimensions). But so purely Hebrew a name for a woman was rare to the point of uniqueness within my own family, and not all that common anywhere else either.

4. A Yiddish contraction of the Hebrew Moshe Yitzkhak, or Moses Isaac, as it would properly be in English.

5. The Yiddish diminutive for the Hebrew Yehudah, or Judah in English.

6. The Yiddish for Pearl, whose Hebrew name, if they had ever given her one, would have been Peninah.

7. Yankl is the Yiddish diminutive for the Hebrew Yaakov, or Jacob, and is hence more or less equivalent to Jackie in English.

8. This was what the Jews called Vilnius.

ACKNOWLEDGMENTS

A few short passages scattered throughout this book were adapted from some of my previously published writings, including essays in *Commentary, National Review,* and *The New Criterion.*

Once again, I wish to express my deep gratitude for the generous support I have received, since retiring as editor-in-chief of *Commentary* in 1995, from the Lynde and Harry Bradley Foundation, the Carthage Foundation, and the John M. Olin Foundation. I am also grateful to the Hudson Institute for appointing me a Senior Fellow and thereby providing me with the time, the resources, and the freedom I needed to write this book. Given that freedom, I and I alone am responsible for the views expressed here, which may or may not be shared, either entirely or in part, by the Hudson Institute or any of the three foundations listed above.

Finally, I owe a great debt to Neal Kozodoy, my successor as editor of *Commentary*, for the suggestions that arose from his brilliantly perspicacious reading of the manuscript. I also wish to thank my agent, Glen Hartley, for forcing me to think harder about a number of important points that struck him when he read an early draft of the manuscript. But most of all, I want to express my gratitude for the support I have received from Chad Conway, my editor at The Free Press, with whom it has been a joy to work at every stage in the publication of this book.

INDEX

INDEX